BEAN *to* BAR CHOCOLATE

AMERICA'S CRAFT CHOCOLATE REVOLUTION
THE ORIGINS • THE MAKERS • THE MIND-BLOWING FLAVORS

MEGAN GILLER
RECIPE PHOTOGRAPHY BY JODY HORTON

Storey Publishing

The mission of Storey Publishing is to serve our customers by
publishing practical information that encourages
personal independence in harmony with the environment.

EDITED BY Hannah Fries and Sarah Guare
ART DIRECTION AND BOOK DESIGN BY Carolyn Eckert
TEXT PRODUCTION BY Erin Dawson
INDEXED BY Christine R. Lindemer, Boston Road Communications

COVER PHOTOGRAPHY BY © Jody Horton, back (bottom), inside back (left); Mars Vilaubi, front,
spine, back (top & bottom right, backgrounds), inside front (spread & facing title page), inside back (right);
William Mullan, back (top left); Courtesy of To'ak, back, (top right & middle); Courtesy of Askinosie
Chocolate, back (bottom left); Sascha Reinking Photography, back (author)

INTERIOR PHOTOGRAPHY CREDITS APPEAR ON PAGE 231

ILLUSTRATIONS BY © Amber Day

© 2017 BY MEGAN GILLER

Storey Publishing
210 MASS MoCA Way
North Adams, MA 01247
storey.com

Printed in China by Toppan Leefung Printing Ltd.
10 9 8 7 6 5 4 3 2 1

Library of Congress Cataloging-in-Publication Data

Names: Giller, Megan, author.
Title: Bean-to-bar chocolate : America's craft
    chocolate revolution : the
    origins, the makers, and the mind-blowing
    flavors / Megan Giller.
Description: North Adams, MA : Storey Publishing,
    [2017] | Includes bibliographical references and
    index.
Identifiers: LCCN 2017024294 (print) |
    LCCN 2017011628 (ebook) |
    ISBN 9781612128214 (paper over board :
    alk. paper) | ISBN 9781612128221 (ebook)
Subjects: LCSH: Chocolate. | Cooking (Chocolate) |
    Cocoa. | LCGFT: Cookbooks.
Classification: LCC TP640 .G55 2017 (ebook) |
    LCC TP640 (print) | DDC
    641.6/374—dc23
LC record available at https://lccn.loc
    .gov/2017024294

TO MARCUS

CONTENTS

FOREWORD

By Michael Laiskonis, Creative Director, Institute of Culinary Education

MAKING CHOCOLATE IS EASY. Making *good* chocolate is extremely difficult.

Most chocolate makers I know share this sentiment to some degree. While a bar of chocolate is indeed the sum of its ingredients and its manufacturing steps, the art and science of crafting that bar also rely on a subtractive process, much like a sculptor liberating beauty from an uncarved block.

The chocolate maker starts with an unroasted cocoa bean — an edible diamond in-the-rough — paring away the superfluous to reveal its essential nature. The resulting flavors are an expression of the bean's time, place, and heritage, and even a bit of the maker's personality. Compounding this already complex task is the skill needed to preserve the taste of the bean — its bitter edges intact — and then steer the process toward showing that bean's potential. It's a skill that relies on experience, endless testing and tasting, and some intuition. The more I learn about chocolate, the more I realize how much I *don't know*, which is both wonderfully satisfying and endlessly frustrating. Alas, the word *craft* itself implies an endless pursuit of elusive perfection.

This is the driving force behind craft chocolate, and this book is the first attempt at chronicling this movement in real time. With a connoisseur's obsession and an investigator's precision, Megan Giller has created a road map for chocolate lovers to better navigate this brave new world of small-scale producers, their processes, and the delicious diversity of their products. Megan's own story is like many others — a happenstance tasting bore a life-changing revelation: not all chocolate is the same. It can be different. What separates craft chocolate from the industrial goes far beyond mere aesthetics and into the philosophical. Craft chocolate embraces the variability of an agricultural product that has subtle differences from one origin to the next, and from harvest to harvest. Each batch — each bar — embodies the cocoa bean's individuality.

As we consumers seek to broaden our palates with the flavors of fine chocolate, we also care deeply about where it's from, what's in it, and how it's made. Insight, which this book offers in great depth, enhances the tasting experience. Ethical sourcing and transparency of the process, too, are increasingly important. One might argue that this homegrown movement and its followers are helping to shift the entire chocolate industry, influencing how the largest chocolate companies approach, or at least market, their own products. This new era of chocolate is

about hunting down the best raw material, respecting its sense of place, and sharing the untold stories of the farmers who make it possible.

As we trace the story of chocolate from its wild origins to its spread across the globe, we discover transformations and refinements along the way. There is romance in the idea that the current craft movement is about taking chocolate back into the realm of a hands-on, artisan aesthetic. Yet this movement is rather a leap forward in chocolate's evolution that simply builds and improves upon its past. As you read the profiles within, you realize no two chocolate makers are alike and thus no two chocolate bars are alike. There is no right or wrong way to make chocolate, and I firmly believe there is little bad chocolate to be had. These personal styles and the strong opinions that guide them ensure an endless opportunity for new chocolate experiences.

Among the many talented experts that Megan introduces in this book is Ed Seguine (former researcher for Guittard and Mars and now an independent adviser). I once attended a panel discussion on the current state of craft chocolate, where he sat as an authoritative anchor of the industry. Regarding the very serious business of tasting fine chocolate, Ed reminded us of one simple truth: "If we aren't having fun, we're doing it wrong." The best chocolate in the world is simply the one you enjoy most. With this book in hand, I encourage you to taste, taste, taste all that this movement has to offer. The best chocolate is always out there, waiting to be discovered.

CHOCOHOLICS
From
CAKE
TO CRAFT
ANONYMOUS

I CONFESS: in the eighth grade, I wrote a poem about chocolate cake. My mom pulled the cake out of the oven, and it was just so, I don't know, *gooey*, sitting there, wafting cocoa scents that would tempt an ascetic. All evidence of that poem has now been destroyed, though it took a lot longer to realize the silliness of my stanzas than it did to scarf a few slices of cake.

My mom didn't seem surprised by the poem. After all, I was the person who, at three years old, invented an ingenious new way to lick the batter out of the bowl: by putting it on my head, with my tongue stretched out to catch the chocolate as the aluminum rotated (spatial intelligence was never my strong suit). After I'd lacquered my hair with batter, my mother threw me into the bath. Needless to say, I ended up with a mouthful of soapy water instead of endless cocoa.

Flash-forward a few decades. I spotted a small chocolate shop in Portland, Oregon, and just had to check it out. When I walked in, though, my heart almost stopped. The walls brimmed with packages so brightly colored they almost bounced off the shelves, jars of sweet-looking nectar beckoned, and a few fulfilled faces sat sipping something dark and dreamy.

"Cacao. Drink chocolate," the store's sign said.

"Yes," I replied.

On that first visit I timidly bought a bar from the huge collection, judging it solely on its pretty wrapper. "Are you sure you don't want to try anything?" the salesperson asked as I retreated into the cool evening.

That night, after devouring all of that delectable chocolate in my Airbnb apartment, I couldn't sleep. And it wasn't from a sugar high. This stuff was different from the Snickers bars and chocolate hearts that I was used to. It was darker, more flavorful, more real. I'd had enough of truffles and candies with creams and fillings. It turns out they mask the real treat: the chocolate.

But what did the guy at Cacao mean when he offered to let me try something?

I couldn't stay away for long. The next day found me waiting at the store when it opened at 10 a.m. My new best friend, co-owner Aubrey Lindley, an effusive, brown-haired 30-something, walked me through bite after bite of chocolate. "This 75 percent Madagascar from Patric is really fruity," he told me as he handed me a square.

I nodded, but he could tell I was lost. "The beans are from Madagascar," he explained. "That country is known for cocoa with a strong, sweet acidity, and Patric knows just what to do with it."

I put the square on my tongue, and under the dominant chocolate flavor, it tasted bright, almost like a raspberry. This wasn't your after-dinner Dove chocolate heart with an inspirational message. Beyond all the complex flavors (even though there were only three ingredients: cocoa, cane sugar, and cocoa butter!), the darkness was different too. Hershey's Special Dark hits only 45 percent cocoa, and this bite measured 75 percent. Still, it tasted smooth, sweet, and creamy, even without any milk.

Aubrey watched my face. "Try a nuttier chocolate," he said, breaking off a piece of Dandelion's bar from Mantuano, Venezuela. I closed my eyes. Roasted nuts. Like the most decadent, tiny fudge brownie that has ever existed.

"What's, like, the weirdest thing you have?" I asked him. Clearly I was getting more comfortable with this whole idea of eating chocolate for free.

Aubrey let out a wild giggle. "This one," he said, pulling an Amano Dos Rios bar off the shelf. "It's like licorice."

It turns out that chocolate, like beer and coffee (and wine, our old snobby friend), holds many different tastes. Berries. Citrus. Nuts. Leather. Grass. A number two pencil. As Aubrey placed different squares side by side, I could taste the entire world in chocolate.

And it's no longer coming only from France or Belgium or even good old neutral Switzerland. American makers now match and even exceed the master-pieces from big European companies like Valrhona and Pralus. This new move-ment of bean-to-bar makers produces bolder, bigger chocolates. Distinctly American chocolates. Just as craft beer and specialty coffee have taken America by storm, with small-batch makers creating products that take taste to a higher level, chocolate is evolving too. We're increasingly turning to the darker stuff to satisfy our more sophisticated palates. Makers of small-batch bars from the bean are *en vogue* from coast to coast, boldly transforming the super-sweet candy bar of your childhood into a grown-up treat. Big companies have started to follow suit, as have a bunch of specialty stores around the country and even regular old grocery stores. In other words, it's the golden age of chocolate.

Two hours later I waddled out of the store with enough theobromine to take out a pack of wild dogs, and with a new determination to find the best of the best. I wish I could say my quest was grounded in some intellectual purpose or humanitarian good, but nope, I just wanted to eat more chocolate.

Back at home, I gleefully cleared out black beans and canned tuna from the pantry's biggest shelf to make room for bars from Askinosie and Dick Taylor and Fruition. Sure, I could eat chocolate until I was brown in the face. But finding the best chocolate from the best makers, and understanding what I was tasting? Well, that was a different story.

This book has grown out of my jour-ney to explore the world of American craft chocolate. After years of learning on my own, I launched a site called Chocolate Noise that cuts through the noise of hype, reviews, and top 10 lists to capture a moment in time, with long-form profiles of the best makers in the

country as well as timely snippets about chocolate today. But I've realized that it's not enough. There isn't a good in-depth guide to the world of craft chocolate.

That's why I've written this book. Each chapter highlights unique aspects of bean-to-bar chocolate and its makers, from the difficulty of roasting beans to the beautiful art on the labels. Read the stories of makers like Dan and Jael Rattigan at French Broad, who drove across the country in an RV converted to run on used vegetable oil in order to start a new chocolate-filled life. They eventually opened the most delectable chocolate café in the country, where you'll find chocolate bars as well as chocolate cake, brownies, ice cream, cookies, truffles, mousse, and more. Or Alan McClure of Patric Chocolate. Though he is already a master of making chocolate, he is so enamored with the science of the stuff that he's working on a graduate degree in food science. Hear about chocolate pioneers like John Scharffenberger and Robert Steinberg of Scharffen Berger Chocolate Maker, who coined the phrase "bean to bar" and inspired a generation of makers, as well as Mott Green of the Grenada Chocolate Company, who after living as a homeless wanderer for years found himself on the beach in Grenada, foraging wild cacao pods. He eventually created a worker-run co-op that sails chocolate around the world.

You'll also find recipes intended to be made with craft chocolate and high-quality cocoa, like the single-origin brownie flight from Dandelion Chocolate, cocoa nib ice cream from James Beard Award–winning cookbook author Alice Medrich, and the grown-up's PB&J truffle from James Beard Award–winning pastry chef Michael Laiskonis. I hope that this book will be a resource for chocolate-crazy people across the country, and the globe.

Because, going back to my favorite book and movie of all time, Charlie was onto something when he chose that solid chocolate bar instead of candy in *Charlie and the Chocolate Factory*. First off, he found his golden ticket. But he also predicted the next big movement in the artisan food world: pure chocolate, made from the bean.

About the
RECIPES
IN THIS BOOK

A FEW YEARS AGO, while eating a bar of bean-to-bar chocolate with my best friend, she asked me a question that changed my life: "What do you do with bars of craft chocolate besides eat them? Like, when you get bored with eating them, is there another way to use them?"

Bored?! With eating *chocolate bars*?

I had never heard of such a thing. But then I started to think about it. I love candy, cakes, and cookies as much as the next person (okay, probably more). What if there was a way to enjoy this new **bean-to-bar chocolate** in other forms besides bars? Some chocolate makers and chocolatiers have started to experiment with making **truffles**, bark, brownies, and other treats out of small-batch chocolate. But I want you to be able to enjoy these at home too.

My favorite pastry chefs, chocolate makers, and chocolatiers designed the recipes in this book so that you will be able to taste the flavor notes of the chocolate in all of their beauty, and you'll often see comments about which origins to use. So the bright, fruity notes of a Madagascar bar will pop in the finished drinking chocolate on page 27, and the deep nutty notes of a Venezuela will sing in the single-origin truffles on page 50. Take those origin notes as suggestions, not orders, and play around with them as much as you like. After all, chocolate should be fun!

Keep in mind that some bean-to-bar chocolate does not have additional cocoa butter. Cocoa butter adds fluidity, so chocolate without added cocoa butter might be thicker when melted and harder to **temper** (see page 11), and possibly a bit harder to work with when making truffles and **bonbons** than **couverture** chocolate (which is made with a high percentage of added cocoa butter). For some of the recipes (like the bonbons), it might make more sense for you to seek out bean-to-bar chocolates made with added cocoa butter (look for it on the ingredients list).

Also, I know that bean-to-bar chocolate is expensive. Making chocolate treats at home is an investment, but I've tried to keep price in mind with these recipes. Some bean-to-bar makers and stores sell chocolate and cocoa powder for baking; check out my list on page 217 of the best places to find bean-to-bar chocolate in bulk.

Most of these recipes are pretty straightforward, with just a few ingredients. That's why it's even more important than usual to use the freshest ingredients you can find, from local sources whenever possible. A simple drinking chocolate will taste even more delicious when it's made with brand-spanking-new whole milk straight off the farm near your house, for instance. The same goes for ice creams, truffles, brownies, and, well, everything. Those ingredients will make high-quality chocolate taste even *more* high quality. And you'll make everyone jealous of your mad baking and chocolatiering skills. In fact, I'm already jealous!

Note that the recipes are rated easy, medium, and advanced. Easy means the recipe is a no-brainer, and I have total faith that you can make it as a beginner. Medium means it's a bit more complicated but still pretty straightforward. Advanced doesn't mean that it's impossible, just that there are many steps or that you need to be hypervigilant about reading the recipe ahead of time. After all, working with chocolate can be a bit tricky. But I believe in you!

To help you get started, the following pages offer a few tips on melting and tempering chocolate. Once you've tempered your chocolate, you're ready to make bonbons and truffles. You'll probably notice that the bonbon recipes in this book have different instructions. I've tried to showcase a range of ways to make them at home. I recommend trying all the methods, picking your favorite, and then applying that to the other recipes.

CHEF'S TIP

Always check the temperature of the oven using a secondary thermometer to make sure your oven temp is accurate. And be sure to let the oven preheat. You want its walls and floor to get hot so that when you open it, the oven doesn't release all of its heat immediately.

MOST OF THE RECIPES in this book call for melting chocolate in some capacity. You can do this in either a double boiler or a microwave. Always start by chopping the chocolate into smaller pieces, and, especially if you're using the double-boiler method, keep it far, far away from any water (if chocolate touches water, it will seize — that is, it will get clumpy).

If you're using a double boiler, bring the water in the bottom pan to a gentle simmer, set the top pan in place, and add the chopped chocolate. Heat, stirring occasionally, until it is melted. Note that if you don't have a double boiler, a stainless steel bowl set over a pan of gently simmering water will work just as well.

If you're microwaving, start with about 30 seconds to 1 minute, depending on the amount of chocolate. Then microwave in 10- to 15-second intervals until the chocolate is almost completely melted. Finish up with 5-second intervals to make sure you don't burn the chocolate.

Heat chopped chocolate in a double boiler.

Stir the chocolate occasionally until it is melted.

I THOUGHT CHOCOLATE was always in a good mood, but it turns out it can lose its temper. (I know, I know, I'm probably the millionth person to make that joke.) What exactly does it mean to temper chocolate, and why is it important? I like artisan candy maker Liddabit Sweets' analogy: To construct a sturdy building, you want to use bricks that are high quality and all roughly the same size. Well, chocolate is partially made of cocoa butter, which is crystalline, and in this case, you want all the crystals to be the right kind and about the same size (Form V, if you want to get technical). This is the effect of tempering. As a result, tempered chocolate will be shelf-stable, with a nice snap and sheen. Untempered chocolate will be dull and mottled and will **bloom** easily.

INGREDIENTS
- 2 pounds chocolate, chopped

EQUIPMENT
- Rubber spatula
- Instant-read digital or infrared thermometer

CHEF'S TIP =

I highly recommend buying an infrared thermometer, which will tell you the temperature of anything (especially chocolate!) in less than a second. An instant-read digital thermometer will also work. Don't make the same mistake I did when I first started working with chocolate: avoid old-school candy thermometers and meat thermometers. Chocolate is finicky and requires exact temperatures, quickly.

BLOOM is a whitish appearance and chalky texture caused by poor storage or care. Sugar bloom is caused by moisture coming into contact with the chocolate; the chocolate will look dusty. Cocoa butter bloom is caused by poor tempering, faulty storage, or changes in temperature; the chocolate will turn powdery gray, white, or tan and feel soft and crumbly. With cocoa butter bloom, the chocolate isn't ruined; it can be remelted and retempered and will be as good as new. With sugar bloom, you're out of luck.

**Seed the melted chocolate (above).
Test with parchment paper (below).**

**So how do you temper chocolate?
I like to use the seeding method, which
involves the following steps.**

1. Start with a cool room (at most 70 to
72°F [21 to 22°C]) and a large amount
of chocolate. The more chocolate you
have, the easier it is to temper. Let's say
2 pounds.

2. You will be melting all of the crystals
(Form V and all others) out of the choc-
olate and starting fresh. To do so, using a
double boiler or a microwave, melt two-
thirds of the chocolate (1⅓ pounds) to:
   Dark chocolate: 113°F (45°C)
   Milk chocolate: 106°F (41°C)
   White chocolate: 104°F (40°C)

3. If you're using a double boiler, remove
it from the heat. "Seed" the melted
chocolate by adding the last third of the
chocolate (⅔ pound) to it. Make sure the
seed chocolate hasn't bloomed and is in
temper. Stir with your spatula until it's all
completely melted and one uniform mass;
it should get super shiny. The seeded
chocolate has all of those Form V crystals
in it, and they're multiplying through the
rest of the chocolate like wildfire as you
stir and the temperature drops. You want
the temperature to reach:
   Dark chocolate: 90°F (32°C)
   Milk chocolate: 88°F (31°C)
   White chocolate: 86°F (30°C)

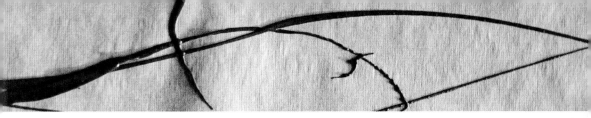

4. At this point, you should have 2 pounds of tempered chocolate to use for bonbons and other confections. Congrats! Test it by dipping half of a small strip of parchment paper in it and letting it cool (scrape the extra chocolate off the piece of paper on the lip of the bowl after you dip). If the chocolate takes a while to dry and sticks to the parchment, it's not tempered (dang!) and you'll have to try again. If it's tempered, it should be shiny and dry quickly; plus, if you touch it, your finger won't leave an imprint. Tempered chocolate should come off the parchment paper easily. Use the tempered chocolate quickly, though it will hold its temperature pretty well — at least long enough for you to use it in mouthwatering recipes like Devil Dogs (page 163) and Single-Origin Dark Chocolate Truffles (page 50).

Troubleshooting

If the melted chocolate has dropped to the appropriate temperature but there are still chunks of unmelted chocolate in your bowl, you have two options: fish them out or place the bowl in the microwave and heat it for 5 to 10 seconds to warm up the chocolate a bit more.

If the temperature is still pretty high and all of your seeds have already melted, you can add a few more. Ideally, though, you want to add them all at once.

ANATOMY OF A
BONBON

THE FILLING

THE SHELL

THE DECORATION

CHAPTER ONE

FROM THE

BEAN

—

IT TURNS OUT that chocolate doesn't appear fully formed out of thin air, a gift from the flavor gods to us gluttons. Instead, it starts as a flower and pod on a *tree*. (While this fact has convinced some people that chocolate is technically salad, this isn't quite the case.) The process of creating chocolate is long, complicated, and, for most people, completely obscured. We mostly know chocolate in its final form, a candy bar, as it makes its way to our open mouth. But over the past 15 years or so, more and more people have started making chocolate from scratch and calling it "bean-to-bar chocolate." To understand what the heck that means, we have to look at other types of chocolate.

WHAT IS BEAN-TO-BAR CHOCOLATE?

ALL CHOCOLATE IS MADE FROM the bean, but *bean-to-bar chocolate* has come to mean something distinct. For contrast, most of the chocolate that we eat is made by big companies. They mix low-quality cocoa beans from all over the world in big batches and then overroast them and add a ton of sugar, vanillin (fake vanilla!), cocoa butter, and emulsifiers like soy lecithin to guarantee that the taste and texture are always the same. What we think chocolate tastes like is usually just sugar and vanilla (but we'll get to that in chapter 3). This type of product is generally called **industrial chocolate**, and though not all of it is bad, it's often a shorthand way of saying that low cost and consistency are the primary goals. Industrial chocolate turns up in many places, especially in the candy bars and chocolate bars we buy at the grocery store and often in the truffles, candies, and bars we buy from chocolatiers.

What's a chocolatier? It's someone who makes candies and confections (think truffles, chocolate bark, and so on). Most of the time chocolatiers buy premade chocolate, melt it down, and use it to make their own bars and confections. Once in a while they make their own chocolate from bean to bar and use that to create confections. Think of a chocolatier as a chef who uses a premade ingredient to create his or her own masterpieces.

"Bean-to-bar chocolate," on the other hand, is made from scratch, usually by a single person or small group of people. (Of course, some big companies make high-quality chocolate: Valrhona, for example, turns out exquisite products that have become the gold standard of pastry chefs and high-end chocolatiers everywhere.) A bean-to-bar chocolate maker sources whole cocoa beans and then roasts, grinds, and smoothens them into chocolate in a single facility. Think of a

Dick Taylor Craft Chocolate sorts cocoa beans by hand to guarantee that only whole, undamaged beans are used.

chocolate maker as an engineer, creating chocolate from the raw materials.

Bean-to-bar chocolate doesn't always taste better than industrial chocolate, but it generally means that the chocolate is made with better ingredients and with a lot of care. Bean-to-bar makers want to celebrate the unique flavors of each type of cocoa and each batch of high-quality beans. They spend a lot of time bringing out those flavor notes and use just enough sugar to bring out the sweetness and creaminess already in the cocoa. That's why almost all bean-to-bar chocolate contains a high percentage of cocoa. A few makers also build their own machines (see pages 35–37 for details!) and pay careful attention to each step in the complicated process.

Many bean-to-bar makers insist on using only cocoa beans and sugar in their chocolate. That's a huge departure from the typical industrial chocolate as well as from European-style chocolate, which uses extra **cocoa butter** to add creaminess and often vanilla to add flavor.

Recently some American makers have started to use cocoa butter and vanilla in their chocolate, though, as well as additions like sea salt and almonds. There's a lot of debate in the community about whether this is a good thing, but in my mind, there's no hard-and-fast rule. For example, Alan McClure of Patric Chocolate, which was the second company in the United States to make **two-ingredient chocolate** and is

Cocoa butter is the fat in a cocoa bean (usually around 50 percent, depending on the bean). Cocoa butter melts at body temperature, which is why it helps create a luxurious, creamy mouthfeel and is often added to bars and bonbons.

widely considered to be one of the best in America, has added cocoa butter to his chocolate for quite some time. As he puts it, "If you can have a delicious 70 percent chocolate bar that has a little bit of added cocoa butter or one that doesn't taste as good or the texture is not as good, are you really going to make the second one because it's more 'pure'? That's just dumb to me." Art Pollard of Amano Artisan Chocolate, one of the original American bean-to-bar companies, which is also considered to be one of the best, has added both cocoa butter and vanilla since the beginning. He said the two-ingredient attitude is all about "ego." Of course, others like Dandelion Chocolate say they create two-ingredient chocolate because that's the type of chocolate that they personally like to eat. I happen to like all of these brands; two ingredients, three ingredients, or more, they all make fantastic chocolate.

One caveat about ingredients, though: you'll almost never see craft makers use industrial emulsifiers, and no one would dream of using a fat or oil besides cocoa butter.

HOW DO YOU MAKE BEAN-TO-BAR CHOCOLATE?

YOU'VE PROBABLY NEVER thought about how that chocolate bar got to be, well, a chocolate bar. And you're not alone: Art Pollard, the owner of Amano Artisan Chocolate, said that he thought "chocolate comes from chocolate" before he started making his own. Turns out it's actually a pretty involved process.

Chocolate's Green Beginnings

It starts at the farm. *Theobroma cacao* trees grow in a range from 20 degrees above to 20 degrees below the equator, and much of the cocoa that bean-to-bar makers use comes from Central and South America. Many makers actually visit the farms themselves and work with farmers to make sure that the cacao is fermented and dried in a way that creates the best possible flavors. Here's how it happens.

1. **PODS GROW.** Cacao flowers grow into pods when tiny insects called midges pollinate them.

2. **FARMERS HARVEST THE BEANS.** The pods are carefully removed from the tree and then opened (sometimes with a machete!). Inside each pod are about 30 cacao "beans" — technically they're seeds — and the farmers scoop them out of the pod. The raw bean itself doesn't taste much like chocolate; that taste will be developed in

processing. In the Caribbean, they call the raw beans "jungle M&Ms," and in every country where cacao grows, people love to eat the tart-sweet pulp that surrounds the beans, which tastes kind of like lychee.

The botanical name for the cacao tree, a tropical evergreen, is *Theobroma cacao*. The genus name, bestowed on it by botanist Carolus Linnaeus, means "food of the gods."

Beans are fermented in their pulp (left); a farmer spreads beans into a thin layer to dry in the sun (right).

3. **THE BEANS ARE FERMENTED.** The beans and pulp are fermented for three to seven days. The sweet pulp attracts microorganisms that launch fermentation. For high-quality chocolate, farmers rigorously monitor the process to ensure that the beans ferment consistently. Some farmers ferment them under banana or plantain leaves or in plastic tents, while others ferment them in wood or plastic boxes. Fermenting the beans removes tannins and makes them less astringent. *This stage is crucial for creating the best flavors possible.* Unfermented beans will not have that signature chocolate taste and will be bitter, and improperly fermented beans will have off-tastes like smoked ham.

4. **THE BEANS ARE DRIED.** In most cases, the wet beans are dried in the sun in a single layer on a concrete patio, on a road, or in a drying shed. After the beans are dried to approximately 7 percent moisture content, they are stable and ready to be made into chocolate!

Many of the tastes we find in chocolate are cemented during the fermenting and drying stages. When beans are fermented and dried correctly, the chocolate flavors come through; when they're not, other flavors (acid, smoke, and so on) overwhelm the chocolate. For example, beans from Papua New Guinea are notorious for their smoky taste. But that's not inherent in the bean. In Papua New Guinea, it rains almost every day. So farmers dry their beans over wood fires, where the smoke seeps into them, changing the flavor. Some call this a defect, but more recently a few makers have started celebrating that distinctive flavor note, like Scott Moore Jr. of Tejas Chocolate, whose smoky bars do well in Texas, the land of barbecue.

Regardless, after this four-step process, the beans are often shipped to other countries for bean-to-bar companies to make into chocolate in their factories at home. But the process is far from over — in fact, it's just getting started!

WHEN ROBERT STEINBERG AND JOHN SCHARFFENBERGER started making chocolate from scratch in 1996 in the Bay Area, they thought it would be a nice "weekend project," John told me recently. Little did they know that they were starting an American revolution and inspiring a generation of bean-to-bar makers. In fact, they coined the term *bean to bar*!

both how good chocolate can be and how frustrating it was that an artisanal company would sell out. They saw the event as the turning point in their careers, when they knew that their passion had to shift from a hobby into a business.

Scharffen Berger's delicious blended bars took off almost immediately, and they soon became a staple of the West Coast scene. In the early 2000s the Hershey Corporation offered to buy Scharffen Berger for much more than the company was worth, and in 2005 they sold to Hershey for about $50 million. Hershey immediately moved the headquarters to Illinois and changed their methods of production.

Many bean-to-bar makers, including Todd Masonis of Dandelion Chocolate, say that this acquisition convinced them they needed to make their own bean-to-bar chocolate. It was a defining moment, revealing

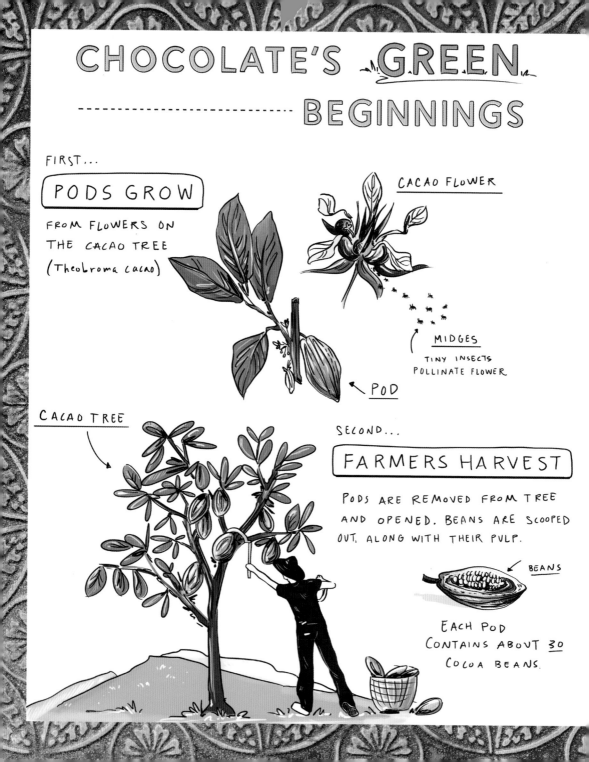

CHOCOLATE'S GREEN BEGINNINGS

FIRST...

PODS GROW

FROM FLOWERS ON THE CACAO TREE (Theobroma cacao)

CACAO FLOWER

MIDGES
TINY INSECTS POLLINATE FLOWER

← POD

CACAO TREE

SECOND...

FARMERS HARVEST

PODS ARE REMOVED FROM TREE AND OPENED. BEANS ARE SCOOPED OUT, ALONG WITH THEIR PULP.

← BEANS

EACH POD CONTAINS ABOUT 30 COCOA BEANS.

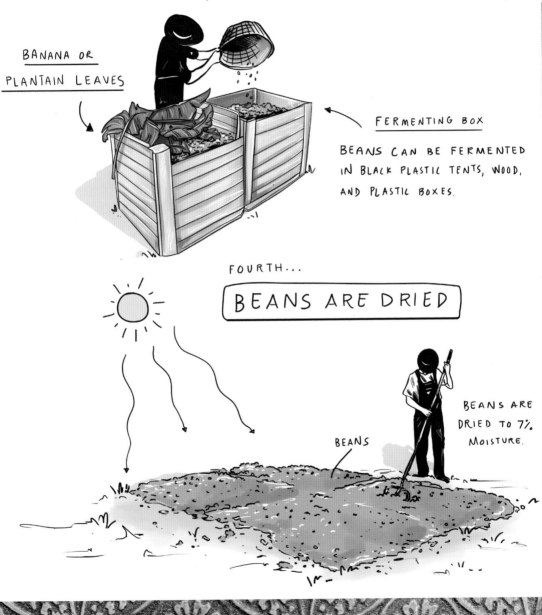

THIRD...

BEANS ARE FERMENTED

(THIS IS WHERE THE BEST FLAVORS ARE CREATED.)

BANANA OR
PLANTAIN LEAVES

FERMENTING BOX

BEANS CAN BE FERMENTED
IN BLACK PLASTIC TENTS, WOOD,
AND PLASTIC BOXES.

FOURTH...

BEANS ARE DRIED

BEANS ARE
DRIED TO 7%
MOISTURE.

BEANS

How Cocoa Beans Become Chocolate

Once the beans find their way into the chocolate maker's hands, it's really time to have some fun. The entire chocolate-making process helps get rid of acidity and off-tastes to bring out the chocolate notes and let other flavors shine. Here's how it works.

1. **ROAST THE BEANS.** Chocolate makers use everything from conventional kitchen ovens to reengineered clothes dryers for roasting, and the temperature and time aren't standardized at all. But the roaster, temperature, and timing hugely affect how the chocolate tastes, so this is one of the most important steps in the chocolate-making process. Almost all chocolate makers roast the beans, though a few have side-stepped this part of the process and choose to make chocolate straight from dried beans.

2. **CRACK, SORT, AND WINNOW.** After roasting, each cocoa bean needs to be cracked to reveal the cocoa nibs inside. The cracked beans are then sorted into nibs and inedible husks in a process called **winnowing**. The husks will be turned into compost or thrown away, while the nibs will become chocolate.

3. **GRIND AND REFINE THE NIBS.** The cocoa nibs are ground into tiny, tiny particles in a machine called a **melangeur** so that the resulting **chocolate "liquor"** is, well, liquidy.

FIRST, COCOA BEANS ARE ROASTED IN AN OVEN OR ROASTER.

THEN, BEANS ARE SORTED, CRACKED...

... AND WINNOWED to SEPARATE THE HUSKS FROM THE NIBS.

COCOA NIBS

CRACKED HUSKS

It's often pretty gritty at this stage, so it's then ground again with sugar and other ingredients, often in machines called roll refiners or ball mills, to make sure all the particles of cocoa, sugar, and anything else are the same tiny micron size. Some makers then use a machine called a **conche** to mix and polish the chocolate and release volatile acids, making it even smoother and more like the European-style chocolate that we're used to eating.

4. **TEMPER**. The final chocolate must be heated and cooled to the correct temperature to have a nice snap and sheen. After this process, the chocolate is shelf-stable and ready to be eaten!

By changing variables like the roasting temperature and the type of machine they use, makers can shape the chocolate and bring out different flavors, creating chocolate that fits their personality (and taste buds).

Cocoa nibs are the broken pieces of the cocoa bean after the bean has been separated from the shell. The nibs can be eaten on their own or ground to make chocolate liquor.

Chocolate liquor refers to the ground-up cocoa nibs, whether in molten liquid or solid block form, without sugar. It is not alcoholic in any way (sorry). Chocolate liquor + any added cocoa butter = cocoa percentage.

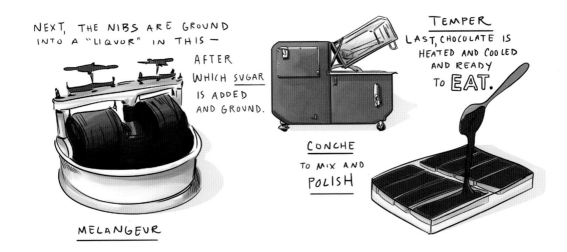

NEXT, THE NIBS ARE GROUND INTO A "LIQUOR" IN THIS —

AFTER WHICH SUGAR IS ADDED AND GROUND.

MELANGEUR

CONCHE TO MIX AND POLISH

TEMPER

LAST, CHOCOLATE IS HEATED AND COOLED AND READY TO EAT.

WHAT'S THE DEAL WITH "CACAO" AND "COCOA"?

AH, THE GREAT DEBATE: Which word do you use when? And will you sound pompous if you use the word *cacao*? I can't answer the second question for you, but I'll try to answer the first. Everyone seems to have a different opinion. For example, chocolate maker Jacques Torres has said that the word *cocoa* means nothing to him, whereas other experts and makers say they prefer the word *cocoa* because it's less intimidating to the uninitiated. Meanwhile, pastry chef and chocolate expert David Lebovitz says in *The Great Book of Chocolate* that *cacao* refers to the pod, the beans, and the paste you make with the beans (also called chocolate liquor). *Cocoa*, on the other hand, refers to the powder made when you press the liquor enough to separate it into cocoa butter and powder.

That might be true, but within the bean-to-bar movement, *cacao* generally refers to the pod and the beans until the beans are finished being fermented and dried. From that point on, it's referred to as *cocoa*. I suspect that the word *cocoa* has developed a bad reputation because it often connotes alkalized cocoa powder (that is, a very processed food). So health food companies have started using *cacao*, even though it's not technically accurate.

It's worth mentioning here that *cocoa* doesn't mean an inferior product; **alkalized cocoa**, sometimes called **Dutched cocoa**, has simply been treated with an alkaline solution. Compared to natural cocoa powder, it's a deeper, darker brown. It's a familiar taste for Americans; think packaged hot chocolate or, in expert Ed Seguine's words, "the essence of an Oreo cookie." **Natural cocoa powder**, on the other hand, has not been processed with alkali. It looks lighter brown than alkalized (Dutch-processed) cocoa and tastes slightly more bitter but has more chocolate flavor.

But honestly, no matter which word you use, everyone will know what you're talking about: something awesome, something chocolate.

Water-Based Drinking Chocolate

LEVEL: *Easy*

Serves

◇ 2 ◇

Recipe from Aubrey Lindley, co-owner of Cacao

YOU MAY HAVE HEARD that water and chocolate don't mix, but this simple recipe from specialty chocolate store Cacao, in Portland, Oregon, proves that old adage wrong. Flavor notes come alive when you melt chocolate and drink it, leaping from subtlety to center stage on your tongue. This recipe will work with any single-origin or dark chocolate blend and is a fun way to try different chocolates. Using water instead of milk or cream intensifies the experience without introducing any other tastes, so you can concentrate on the chocolate goodness. I like it served warm, like a cup of tea.

1½   cups water
8½   ounces dark chocolate
       (68 to 75 percent cocoa), chopped

1. Bring the water to a boil in a small pan. Remove from the heat and add the chocolate. Cover and let sit for 30 to 45 seconds.

2. Whisk gently and scrape the bottom of the pan with a rubber spatula to make sure the chocolate isn't stuck to it. Put the pan back on the burner (keep it turned off) and let rest until the chocolate is completely melted, 2 to 3 minutes.

3. Whisk vigorously for a minute or two to emulsify completely. Check the consistency by seeing if it sticks to the back of a clean spoon. If it is lumpy, keep mixing. If it sticks and is smooth, you are finished. Don't confuse bubbles for clumps; small air bubbles are okay! Some bits of chocolate will stubbornly remain at the bottom of the pan, but don't worry about them.

4. Serve warm. The flavors and texture will evolve as it gradually cools and rests.

Cocoa Tea

Recipe from Miss Choco

LEVEL: *Easy*

Serves

1

VISITED A CUTE LITTLE CHOCOLATE shop in Montreal a few years ago called La Tablette de Miss Choco and found a wealth of craft bars as well as knowledge. Miss Choco (otherwise known as Karine C. Guillemette) walked me through some of the best bars on the market and the stories of their makers. She also pressed a delightful cold drink into my hands: subtle, fruity, and refreshing in the unprecedentedly hot Montreal summer. Turned out it was iced cocoa tea!

You may have seen a few recipes for the stuff, but it was my first introduction, so this version holds a special place in my heart. Drink it hot in the winter or cold in the summer. Experiment with nibs from different origins to find flavor notes that you like best, but be sure to use the highest quality, since they are really the only ingredient (besides water) in this "recipe." Makers like Askinosie, Taza, TCHO, and others sell nibs in specialty stores, some grocery stores, and online.

For a nice variation, steep the nibs with a few fresh mint leaves or raspberries.

1 cup boiling water

1 or 2 tablespoons roasted nibs

Sugar, to taste

FOR HOT TEA

1. Pour the boiling water over 1 tablespoon of nibs. Cover and let steep for 4 to 6 minutes.

2. Strain and sweeten with sugar as desired.

FOR COLD TEA

1. Pour the boiling water over 2 tablespoons of nibs. Cover and let steep for 4 to 6 minutes.

2. Strain and sweeten with sugar as desired, then pour over ice.

THE CRAFT MOVEMENT

THE CHOCOLATE-MAKING process seems pretty complicated. So why in the world are so many people making their own chocolate from scratch?

Ask any craft chocolate makers or lovers what got them hooked on bean-to-bar chocolate and they'll respond with one word: Madagascar. Cocoa from that country is known for its fruity flavors like citrus and red berries — not exactly what you expect to find in chocolate. "That bean single-handedly started the craft movement," Gary Guittard, the fourth-generation owner of Guittard Chocolate, told me. "It's what made people say, 'Wow, what is *this*?'" When Scharffen Berger started selling bars made with cocoa from Madagascar in the late 1990s, food lovers sat up and took notice. They realized that chocolate isn't the flat, boring product mass-produced by industrial companies. And that made them want to create their own chocolate from scratch, with big, bold flavors that challenge our idea of what chocolate tastes like.

Of course, the craft chocolate movement is part of a larger DIY food movement. First we had fine wine, then specialty coffee, then craft beer, now chocolate. People want to be as involved as possible with their food, from buying locally made products to actually making that food themselves. By starting their own businesses and using their own two hands to create something delicious, people are finding connections to the land, their body, and their community. And by controlling the entire process — from bean to bar — makers can create even better-tasting chocolate. They can have a say in the way the beans are fermented, dried, roasted, and so on, as well as in how farmers are treated, creating a process and a product that are uniquely devoted to high standards.

In the past few years, the craft chocolate movement has exploded. Fifteen years ago there were only about 5 bean-to-bar makers in the country, but now there are over 200! Experts only expect that number to keep growing, though many will tell you that they expect to see makers selling more confections instead of straight-up single-origin bars. If wine, beer, and coffee are any indicator (and they are), in 50 years, nuanced, flavorful chocolate bars made locally will be the norm, not the exception.

BLACK FIG
72% MADAGASCAR

Dick Taylor
CRAFT CHOCOLATE

Craft chocolate is a messy term without an agreed-upon definition. According to the now-defunct Craft Chocolate Makers of America, craft chocolate is made from scratch by an independent, small company (one that uses between 1 metric ton and 200 metric tons of cocoa beans per year and is at least 75 percent owned by the company itself or the company's employees). The main concern is not consistency but artfulness and deliciousness. Within the world of chocolate, the term is often interchangeable with *bean to bar*.

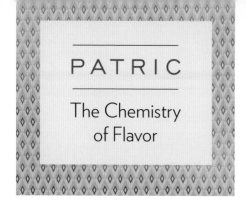

PATRIC

The Chemistry of Flavor

AT AGE 35, ALAN "PATRIC" McCLURE voluntarily enrolled in an organic chemistry class. For nine years, his company, Patric Chocolate, had been widely accepted as one of the best in America. It had won accolades from *Gourmet*, *The New Yorker*, and *Food & Wine*, among others, and a slew of awards at the Northwest Chocolate Festival, the International Chocolate Awards, and Good Food Awards (more than any artisan in any category), captivating chocolate lovers everywhere.

Yet Alan wasn't satisfied. He'd been scouring chemistry books on his own, trying to learn more about flavor formation and texture in chocolate, but he was frustrated at the slow going. So he sought out a professor in flavor chemistry at the University of Missouri to explain a few things. The professor helped

quite a bit, but he didn't know much about chocolate. Rather than give up, Alan went all in: he enrolled in a master's program in food science with an emphasis in flavor chemistry. "I thought, what if I could bring both worlds together? That would create a monster in a positive way in understanding how to tweak chocolate so that the result is even more delicious than anything that's existed before," he said.

Of course, that also meant making some changes in his bean-to-bar chocolate company. As employees left, he didn't replace them, which meant his staff dwindled from five people to two. He reduced production 75 percent, raised his prices, and told his loyal followers what he was up to. "It seemed like a crazy thing to do, but I don't think I had a single person tell

me I was an idiot," he said. Now, if you want a bar from Patric, you have to subscribe to his newsletter, where he announces the releases once per month, and then jump on it faster than a hipster on a fixie bike.

Why not? After all, Patric Chocolate had just started making money in 2013, a rare occurrence for a bean-to-bar company. Going back to school was a risky move. But most people in this industry know that if you could cut down on the trial and error inherent in making craft chocolate (figuring out the right roasting temperature for each batch of beans, deciding how long to conche, and so on) by understanding the chemistry behind it — well, the sky would be the limit. "I had to struggle the whole time to understand more about what I'm doing, the levers and dials that you pull as a chocolate maker," Alan said about what it was like to make chocolate before grad school. "Understanding scientific ways of approaching things has allowed me to have more solid results when I'm doing my own R&D," he continued. "My decisions tend to be better, based on facts" rather than on a hunch.

Alan is already using his new knowledge to make a difference. For example, he's spent the past few years of his graduate work analyzing different cocoa samples to evaluate their levels of **theobromine**, caffeine, and **epicatechin**. Those three compounds, among others, give chocolate its signature bitter taste, one that turns many people off dark chocolate. "I've been looking at the amounts of those in different origins of cocoa in an effort to learn more about exactly where the bitterness is coming

continued on next page

TRIPLE GINGER

DARK MILK

58% COCOA

from," he explained. By analyzing the amounts of each in different types of cocoas, he can better understand how to make less-bitter chocolate from all sorts of beans. In fact, Alan's project has become so big and groundbreaking that at the beginning of 2017, he and his adviser decided to extend it: Alan opted to pursue a PhD in food science.

Because for Patric Chocolate, it all comes back to flavor. Alan makes chocolate that he wants to eat, something that's "not only complex and interesting, but also delicious. I have no use for an interesting bar that doesn't make me want to eat it," he said. "If one taste is enough to last me the rest of my life, then I don't care how complex or unique the bar is. It has to be delicious."

JOHN NANCI, DIY MACHINES, AND AMERICAN INGENUITY

TWENTY YEARS AGO, it was almost impossible to make chocolate on a small scale, because the machines you needed were all expensive, industrial-scale models. Some companies with capital, like Scharffen Berger and Theo, were able to invest in those machines (which can run about $70,000). Individuals who were interested in making chocolate at home were out of luck. That is, until a retired chemist named John Nanci hacked the entire process.

John Nanci considers himself the father of the American bean-to-bar movement, and with good reason. Starting in 2005, he took a bunch of machines made for different purposes and jury-rigged them to work for small-batch chocolate. Now he sells those machines, other inventions, and beans in small quantities, all for reasonable prices. Selling beans in small quantities was itself a revolution in the industry; now anyone could be a chocolate maker without spending thousands of dollars.

Almost every bean-to-bar maker in the country got his start using John's beans and methods, which he publishes on his site, Chocolate Alchemy. Some bigger makers like Raaka still use machines that John invented and produced. Meanwhile, on the other end of the spectrum, almost half of his customers buy machines and beans to make chocolate at home for themselves, not to sell.

Almost all bean-to-bar makers get started by following John Nanci's online advice.

Many winnowers at bean-to-bar factories are DIY, like this one at Dandelion Chocolate.

When most makers get started, they roast beans in batches as small as 1 to 2 pounds.

John will tell you that this business model was his goal from the beginning. He'd seen the craft beer and specialty coffee industries take off, and when he learned about making chocolate from scratch, "it clicked," he said. "I was like, 'I'm not missing this boat.'"

This way of making chocolate — in small batches, with jury-rigged machines — has completely transformed the industry, disrupting the market by allowing people to make and sell their own chocolate rather than relying on premade chocolate from big companies. But some are critical of Nanci's methods. It's hard to earn a living from selling chocolate made this way, because it's hard to scale up and jump to the next size of machinery (commercial equipment). And many experts criticize the texture and taste of chocolate made in granite wet grinders like CocoaTown's. Clay Gordon, founder of the online forum The Chocolate Life and the author of *Discover Chocolate*, claims he can actually *taste* the granite in the resulting chocolate!

Meanwhile, other makers use antique machines that they've refurbished and restored. Amano, for example, uses a massive vintage wooden winnower from the 1920s or 30s. Some people take it one step further and build their own machines. Patric Chocolate, for example, uses a mill originally intended to crack barley at breweries; owner Alan McClure retrofitted it to crack cocoa beans. Most chocolate makers also construct their own winnowing machines, usually with a Shop-Vac and some duct tape, or with a PVC pipe and a vacuum. Rogue Chocolatier's Colin Gasko told me that he and his father (who has a PhD in theoretical physics) built his winnower over the course of a year and a half; it's "MacGyver, built from components that don't have anything to do with winnowing."

As the field develops, makers will iron out these kinks and develop even better methods for creating bean-to-bar chocolate as well as successful business models. For the moment, though, many are starting completely from scratch, figuring out everything from the best roasting temperatures and times to how long to grind and refine their chocolate for the perfect taste. It's no coincidence that a crucial part of the artisan movement is "art": Makers need more than machines to transform bitter cocoa beans and granulated sugar to that ambrosial end product. "It's like with photography," said Aubrey Lindley, co-owner of specialty chocolate store Cacao, in Portland, Oregon. "Something magic happens in the darkroom."

CHOCOLATE MACHINES

Here are some of the bizarre machines John Nanci and others have borrowed, modified, or built from scratch to make chocolate.

JUICER. Used to crack cocoa beans open

CRANKANDSTEIN. Used to crack cocoa beans open

HAIR DRYER. Used to winnow the cracked cocoa beans; the light shell will blow away, leaving the nibs

SHOP-VAC. Used as part of a DIY winnower to separate cocoa nibs from shell

WET GRINDER. Used instead of a traditional melangeur to grind and refine cocoa beans and sugar; one common brand comes from CocoaTown

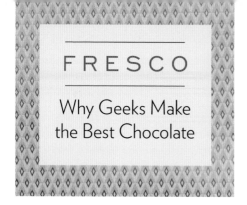

FRESCO

Why Geeks Make the Best Chocolate

ROB ANDERSON IS A GEEK. So he makes chocolate for other geeks, or, more accurately, "people who really like chocolate and geek out about it." What does he mean by that? If you change one step of the chocolate-making process, you change the taste of the resulting chocolate entirely. Rob wants to show you exactly what that means. He roasts beans three different ways and conches chocolate four different ways to create unique bars that bring the eater into the factory to be part of the process. Oh, and did I mention that he built most of the machines he uses?

First, let's talk terms. Most people understand the concept of roasting cocoa beans, whether that's done in a convection oven or, in Rob's case, a modified commercial clothes dryer ("I was like, 'Oh my gosh, this is perfect,'" he recalls on finding it). But conching? What

the heck is conching? After the beans are ground and refined with sugar and sometimes cocoa butter, the resulting chocolate can still be kind of grainy. Some makers, especially those making European-style chocolate, add an extra step in the chocolate-making process and put the liquor in a machine called a conche, which stirs, aerates, and heats it in a particular way to make it extra smooth and bring out the best flavors even further.

There are many types of conches, and everyone has his or her own opinion about which is the best. Rob will tell you just about anything you want to know — unless it's about his conche, which he built himself. That's proprietary information. "That's my intellectual piece that keeps me apart from some other [makers]," he explained. "Applying the right amount of heat, aeration, and time to balance

flavors for each cocoa origin and harvest can be challenging but exceptionally rewarding when the results are good."

Of course, that's easier said than done. Over 15 years, Rob's roaster has gone through at least four iterations, the winnower over a dozen, the conche four. It turns out it's actually pretty hard to make great chocolate. And just because you have a good machine doesn't mean you can make good chocolate. It's all about how you *use* those machines. Rob roasts beans three different ways:

- **LIGHT.** "Just enough to soften raw cocoa's acidic or green edge"

- **MEDIUM.** "Cocoa flavors develop to be balanced and flavorful"

- **DARK.** "Full bodied, bold, intense; new flavor notes can develop while others may be subdued"

And he conches the chocolate four different ways:

- **NONE.** "Primitive, natural, pungent, not appropriate for all cocoa, exquisite for some"

- **SUBTLE.** "Softens primitive edge while retaining aggressive flavor notes"

- **MEDIUM.** "A mellow balance between aggressive and subdued"

- **LONG.** "Flavor peaks and valleys softened to a melodic harmony"

Most people have a house style, and you can either take it or leave it. Rob gives you a choice. Do you want a dark roast and long conche like the Marañón 230 from Peru? A light roast and no conche like the Papua New Guinea 222? Or would you prefer a medium roast and medium conche like the Dominican Republic 224 (which won a gold award at the 2015 International Chocolate Awards)?

Now, all of these factors change the way the chocolate tastes immensely — and we haven't even started to talk about *terroir*, or the idea that the taste of the cocoa is affected by the soil, landscape, and environment in which it's grown (see chapter 2). That's Rob's next project. As predicted, he's getting super geeky about it. Like most makers, he already lists the cocoa's country of origin and the year it was made into chocolate on his label. But now he's comparing not only different countries but also different harvests. "I've got chocolate that is made with beans from two consecutive harvest years," he told me recently. "I am going to be doing a compare and contrast with chocolate made exactly the same but with beans from two different harvest seasons." So if it rained more one season than the next, for example, you'll be able to taste the difference in your chocolate bar. As far as I know, no one has done an experiment quite like this before. But if there's one man for the job, it's Rob.

Cocoa Nib Ice Cream

Recipe from *Seriously Bitter Sweet*, by Alice Medrich, James Beard Award–winning cookbook author, pastry chef, and chocolatier

LEVEL: *Easy*

Yield

About 3½ cups

'VE BEEN A FAN of baker and chocolatier Alice Medrich since before I was born. Back in the 1970s in Berkeley, my parents stuffed their faces with chocolate at her café, Cocolat (which is best known for introducing America to truffles), and the Cocolat cookbook is still one of their most prized possessions.

That's why I'm so excited to include this recipe from her. It reinvents chocolate ice cream by steeping the base with cocoa nibs, which creates an underlying chocolate flavor that she says is "somehow both subtle and dramatic." It also highlights an essential element of the chocolate-making process, the roasted nib, which is why it's one of my favorite recipes in this book.

Use local cream and milk, if you can get them, and high-quality nibs, since they are the backbone of this recipe. For some added crunch, try mixing a few tablespoons of fresh nibs into the ice cream when it's finished, or sprinkling some on top.

1½   cups heavy cream
1½   cups whole milk
½   cup sugar
⅓   cup roasted cocoa nibs
⅛   teaspoon salt

SPECIAL EQUIPMENT
Ice cream maker

1. Bring the cream, milk, sugar, nibs, and salt to a boil in a medium saucepan over medium heat. Remove from the heat, cover, and let steep for 20 minutes.

2. Pour the cream mixture through a fine-mesh strainer into a bowl, pressing on the nibs to extract all the liquid. Discard the nibs. Refrigerate the cream, covered, until thoroughly chilled (a few hours).

3. Freeze the mixture according to the instructions for your ice cream maker.

THAT TIME I TRIED MY HAND AT MAKING CHOCOLATE

T SEEMED SIMPLE ENOUGH: roast the beans, crack the beans, remove the husks, grind the nibs with sugar, then temper the chocolate and form it into bars. I had described how to make chocolate from scratch many times, but I'd never put nibs to the grindstone myself. And that's how I came to be standing on my neighbor's porch hair-drying a bowl of cracked cocoa beans, covered in husk from head to toe.

"I can totally do this," I told my husband the night before. I was planning to make 70 percent Ecuador chocolate. When he came home from work the next day, I was hunched by the oven, my ear pressed against the glass window.

"What are you doing?" he asked.

"I'm listening for popping cocoa beans!" I said. "Does it smell like brownies? Does it SMELL LIKE BROWNIES?"

Popping and that brownie aroma are the two telltale signs that beans are finished roasting, and though they seemed easy to identify in theory, well, I was having trouble. Eventually I pulled the beans out of the oven, cracked one open, and compared it to some French Broad roasted nibs from Nicaragua. French Broad's had a deep, rich flavor; mine tasted like sour red wine. Great. I was off to a solid start.

The next day, I got started with a borrowed **Crankandstein** to crack the beans. It's a giant metal funnel attached to a couple of pieces of plywood and a hand-cranked roller, with a square cut out of the bottom for the cracked beans to fall through. I'd heard about this thing for years, and in person it was even more DIY than I'd imagined. After putting the plywood base over a small bucket and filling the funnel with beans, I started cranking the handle. The force caused it to jump away from me. After a few false starts, I eventually figured it out: if I jammed the plywood base into my side and held on to it with one hand, I could use the other hand to turn the crank somewhat jerkily as cracked beans made their way through the machine. Five minutes and I was finished.

Then the real fun started. Most makers construct their own winnower to remove the husks from the nibs, but if you're just getting started, you use a hair dryer. "You'll have about a six-foot circle of husk around you," John Nanci writes on his site Chocolate Alchemy. After failing to find an outlet outside, my plan had been to take a bowl of cracked beans and a hair dryer into the shower and draw the curtain, since my husband had more than intimated that he would indeed kill me if I destroyed our house.

Thankfully, our neighbor agreed to let me borrow her porch ("It makes a huge mess, and can I use your backyard?" my text read). I'd seen someone do this before: you shake the bowl as you vibrate the hair dryer over it. After an hour I'd blown away almost half the mass and was still finding big pieces of shell. "It looks good enough," my neighbor said.

Next I threw handfuls of the nibs into a borrowed wet grinder that Nanci had modified so people could use it as a melangeur to grind and refine nibs. It's basically a granite bowl with two granite wheels spinning inside it. I could have added extra cocoa butter to make the texture creamier; I could have poured in some vanilla to smooth out the taste. But I was making true American-style chocolate, which meant only two ingredients: cocoa and sugar. The clamor of the machine's grating overwhelmed my tiny apartment, sending my poor dog running from room to room in search of solace. Eventually I stuck it in a closet to do its work. (Side note: I've also made ice cream in that closet. Oh, Brooklyn.)

After 30 hours — yes, 30 whole hours — I decided I'd go crazy if I had to listen to that machine for one more minute. My dog agreed.

I transferred the chocolate to ice cube trays to rest for a few days.

"Whew," I thought. "The hard part is over."

Uh, right. Turns out tempering by hand on a stainless steel countertop while your husband isn't looking is actually pretty tricky, especially when you've never done it before. Especially when your chocolate smells like freezer burn because you stored the stuff in ice cube trays. On my second attempt, the chocolate looked shiny and started to set (victory!), so I quickly transferred it to a makeshift mold in a Tupperware top. Within minutes it had bloomed: white cocoa butter marbled the mottled surface of the dull chocolate.

But . . . I had made chocolate! I tasted it. Brittle, bitter. It coated my mouth like latex. There was something crunchy in the middle. I looked longingly at my kitchen cabinet, where I kept my chocolate stash, then threw in the towel, made a mad dash for some Patric and took a bite, letting it melt while the flavor notes sang their complex melody.

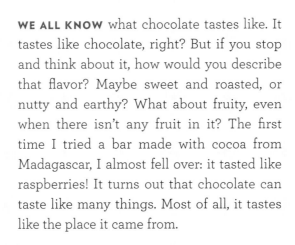

CHAPTER TWO

A SENSE OF PLACE

WE ALL KNOW what chocolate tastes like. It tastes like chocolate, right? But if you stop and think about it, how would you describe that flavor? Maybe sweet and roasted, or nutty and earthy? What about fruity, even when there isn't any fruit in it? The first time I tried a bar made with cocoa from Madagascar, I almost fell over: it tasted like raspberries! It turns out that chocolate can taste like many things. Most of all, it tastes like the place it came from.

WHAT IS SINGLE-ORIGIN CHOCOLATE?

IKE WITH WINE and its grapes, chocolate's taste is partially determined by the environment in which the cacao trees grow. Cocoa beans from different regions have their own distinctive flavors. For example, as I discovered early on, cocoa from Madagascar often tastes fruity, whereas cocoa from Venezuela has a nuttier profile. In the snooty food world, this is called **terroir**.

It means the taste of the beans is affected by the soil, landscape, and environment in which they're grown. In fact, those fruity notes we often taste in chocolate are the direct result of terroir. (By the way, terroir affects not only wine and chocolate but also coffee, cheese, tobacco, and even maple syrup, among other foods.)

Most of us don't usually put chocolate in the same category as wine or

Single-origin chocolate is made using cocoa beans from one specific place, or "origin." The chocolate can be made from a single variety or a blend of varieties, as long as they're from the same location. Note that right now, single origin doesn't mean that the sugar and other ingredients in the chocolate are also from the same origin.

coffee, though, and we expect every chocolate bar to taste the same. That's because over the past hundred years or so, chocolate-making companies have worked hard to standardize the taste, using a blend of beans and adding a ton of other ingredients to mask any bitterness or distinctive flavors (some companies like Hershey and Mars even have proprietary blends!). What most of us know as chocolate is really just sugar and vanilla.

That's where bean-to-bar makers come in. As we saw in the last chapter, *bean to bar* technically means that the maker oversees the entire process, from buying beans to roasting them to grinding them and turning them into chocolate. But in practice this means that people spend a lot of time and care creating a unique chocolate. Instead of creating a uniform product, they strive to bring out the different flavors of each bean to maximize taste and make something special. Most of them create bars using beans from one country in order to concentrate on the terroir of that particular bean (some even use beans from just one farm!). This kind of chocolate is called **single origin**, a term you might already know if you're a coffee connoisseur or a wine aficionado. French company Valrhona pioneered the focus on origins in the 1990s. Not all bean-to-bar chocolate is single origin, but many makers specialize in single-origin bars because they want to highlight the

inherent flavors in the cocoa. (How do they highlight those flavors? Through the bean-to-bar production process, detailed in chapter 1.)

Many makers will designate not only the country of origin but also a specific area within that country. For example, in Venezuela, you'll find amazing beans from the Ocumare region as well as the Maracaibo region. When you see that kind of detail on the label, it often means makers have personally visited that area, worked with farmers, and acquired the beans themselves.

Single-origin Madagascar bar from Patric Chocolate

Blended bar from Raaka using cocoa from the Dominican Republic and Bolivia

Some people take this idea even further and make **single-estate** chocolate. That means the beans come from not just one particular location but one particular farm within that location. This almost always means the maker has spent extensive time at the farm (and sometimes, in the case of bigger companies like Valrhona and even tiny ones like Lonohana, it means they actually own the farm!). They'll be able to tell you how one harvest tastes different from another and why, and they'll be able to give you tons of details about the farmers' lives and how they worked with and processed the beans. The more they dial down to a specific country, area, and farm, the more they're able to control the way the chocolate tastes. Of course, the single-estate designation doesn't guarantee that the resulting chocolate will taste good, but it's often an indicator. When you see a single-estate chocolate, know that you're most likely eating something special.

The terms *single origin* and even *single estate* don't mean that the chocolate is being made in the country where the beans are sourced. Most makers buy beans from farmers in other countries and ship them back to their factories in the United States or Europe. There are exceptions, of course: Pacari makes fantastic raw chocolate in Ecuador, and Marou makes amazing bars in Vietnam.

Although the term *single-origin chocolate* is new, people have been categorizing the sweet stuff by location for hundreds of years. The Aztecs organized their supplies of cocoa beans according to where they were grown, and in the late 1700s, Peruvians even considered creating official fixed prices for cocoa beans based on origin and quality. With the industrial era, the concept of classifying cocoa this way faded — perhaps, as I mentioned above, because at first bigger companies simply wanted to keep their recipes secret, but over time some began blending lower-quality beans from many different locations and overroasting them to disguise their acidity and bitterness and create a uniform product.

Keep in mind that not all good chocolate is single origin, and not all single-origin chocolate is necessarily good. Some people overlook this, as Alan McClure of Patric Chocolate knows all too well. When he first started making a blended bar in 2010 (one of the first craft **blends** in the country!), some wholesale customers "not only wouldn't order some of the blend and flavored bars but didn't even want a sample of them to consider, and all because they were not single origin," he recalled recently. "[Blends were] a risky thing to do." Yet blends of high-quality chocolate (in other words, chocolate made with more than one variety of cocoa) can be delicious and sometimes more balanced than single-origin chocolate. On the opposite end, single-origin chocolate clumsily made with poor-quality beans won't taste good.

However, as a general rule, if your chocolate is made with single-origin, fine-flavor beans, you're looking at some carefully crafted chocolate. That's because the maker has taken time to taste all the flavors in the beans and bring them out in interesting ways. What kinds of flavors? Beyond sweet, nutty, and roasted, think fruity, floral, earthy, dairy, and spicy. And on and on!

At Fond Doux Plantation in Saint Lucia, beans are dried in the sun in between rain showers.

Single-Origin Dark Chocolate Truffles

Recipe from Fruition Chocolate
(read more about them on page 118!)

LEVEL:
Advanced

Yield

**50 to 55
gumball-size
truffles**

LATELY I'VE TASTED some amazing creations from chocolate makers and chocolatiers. They're taking bean-to-bar, single-origin chocolate and transforming it into creamy, decadent truffles. Eat one and you can still taste the particular flavor notes of the cocoa. It's a huge departure from the blended chocolate used to make truffles and candies in the past, and it's a fun and different way to enjoy single-origin chocolate. That's why I asked Fruition Chocolate, one of my favorite makers in the country, to contribute this recipe.

Glucose syrup may seem like a weird ingredient, but it's a vital one here. Buy it at high-end baking and specialty food stores and — of course — online. The most common type is DE-44, but any will do. Also, for this recipe, you want to soften and cream the butter; it should look like whipped butter before you add it to the **ganache**.

FOR THE GANACHE

12¼ ounces single-origin dark chocolate (65 to 85 percent cocoa)

7 ounces heavy cream

1 tablespoon glucose syrup

3¾ tablespoons room-temperature butter, whipped

TO COAT THE TRUFFLES

1 pound single-origin dark chocolate (65 to 85 percent cocoa)

SPECIAL EQUIPMENT

Pastry bag (for a DIY version, see Chef's Tips, page 60), food processor

1. For the ganache, place the 12¼ ounces of chocolate in a food processor and pulse several times to break it into small pieces. Leave the chocolate in the bowl of the processor.

2. Pour the heavy cream and glucose syrup into a large saucepan and heat on low until the mixture reaches a rolling boil.

3. With the top of the processor on and the motor running, pour the hot cream into the chocolate and process until the mixture is emulsified. This should take about a minute. The ganache will be shiny and smooth when it's ready, like pudding.

4. Let the ganache cool a bit (to 95°F [35°C], if you want to get technical), then add the butter into the food processor and blend. (If it's too hot, the butter will break and the ganache will no longer be emulsified.) Now let the ganache cool for about 15 minutes, until it reaches 85°F (29°C).

5. Line a baking sheet with parchment paper. Transfer the ganache to a pastry bag and pipe into quarter-size balls on the baking sheet. As you pipe, keep the bag about ¼ inch above the paper so it doesn't touch or stick to the paper. Cover the balls with plastic wrap and place in the refrigerator overnight to firm.

6. The next day, using your hands, roll each rough ball into a more-rounded ball. Some people like to wear gloves here, because this step is kind of sticky and messy. (Sorry, not sorry.)

7. For the chocolate coating, temper the pound of chocolate, following the instructions on page 11.

recipe continues on next page

STEP 6

CHEF'S TIP

Ganache should look well mixed and shiny, like chocolate pudding. If it starts to look greasy, like the ingredients are separating (this is called "broken ganache" in the industry), put it back in the food processor for another whirl or stir briskly with a spatula until it's reemulsified.

Single-Origin
Dark Chocolate
Truffles continued

STEP 8

8. Line a baking sheet with parchment paper. While the tempered chocolate is still warm, drop each ganache ball, one at a time, into it. Using a fork to guide it, roll the ball over once so that it's completely coated in the melted chocolate. Balance it on the fork, bouncing or shaking it lightly to remove any extra chocolate, then wipe the bottom of the fork against the edge of the bowl to remove any remaining extra chocolate. Place on the lined baking sheet.

9. Let the truffles sit at room temperature until the chocolate coating is set, which should take 5 minutes or less. Enjoy! (Oh, and if for some reason you can't eat 50 truffles in one sitting, check out Chef's Tips, page 60, for instructions on how to store them.)

STEVE DEVRIES

STEVE DEVRIES might just make the best chocolate in the world, but unfortunately, you can't buy it. Of course, he had his own company for 10 years: DeVries Chocolate, which opened in 2005 with the tagline "100 Years Behind the Times" and is still famous for its exquisite bars and caramelized nib clusters. He was the first person in the country to make two-ingredient chocolate. By 2008, the *New York Times, Los Angeles Times, Washington Post,* and *Saveur* had all lauded his work. But when the recession hit, like many people, Steve started having trouble, and in 2015 he shut down production.

The mustachioed, friendly 60-something has been focusing on leading tours for Ecole Chocolat and others to cacao-producing countries, as he did in the years before closing his business. He teaches the locals there how to ferment and dry cacao beans to make the best possible chocolate (pretty much every great maker in the country, from Dandelion to Ritual, has traveled with him). He also consults for chocolate companies, is building one of the largest chocolate book libraries in the world, and generally inspires the bean-to-bar world as a living legend.

WHERE AMERICAN CHOCOLATE COMES FROM —
And What It Tastes Like

When I first started trying craft chocolate, I desperately wanted a guide to tell me what each country's beans taste like so I could find my favorites. I looked high and low but couldn't find anything to help. But you're in luck: this cheat sheet gives you overall taste descriptions of each country's beans. There are dozens of other flavors to find in the beans, but these are the predominant ones.

CEAN

ASIA

EUROPE

EQUATOR

CACAO ONLY GROWS 20 DEGREES NORTH AND SOUTH OF THE EQUATOR

AFRICA

PHILIPPINES
EARTHY

TANZANIA
ROASTY

VIETNAM
FRUITY, SPICY

INDIAN OCEAN

MADAGASCAR
FRUITY

PAPUA NEW GUINEA
SMOKY

AUSTRALIA

Grown-Up Peanut Butter and Jelly Truffles

LEVEL:
Advanced

Yield

Approximately 50 truffles

Recipe from Michael Laiskonis, James Beard Award–winning pastry chef and creative director of the Institute of Culinary Education (read more about him on page 182!)

SINGLE-ORIGIN MADAGASCAR chocolate can be a shock: It's bright and fruity, different from the dark, nutty flavors we generally associate with chocolate. Sometimes it can taste like citrus, other times like red berries. Famed pastry chef Michael Laiskonis takes advantage of these flavor notes in this refined truffle, creating a playful riff on two classic combinations: chocolate and peanut butter as well as peanut butter and jelly. This recipe would also work well with chocolate made from other fruity types of cocoa, like what you'd find from Hawaii or Peru. You'll want to use chocolate made with some added cocoa butter (called couverture), which will make it easier to cast the chocolate molds.

Gianduja is a fancy word for a chocolate-nut spread (you've probably heard of the most common brand, Nutella). Usually it's made with hazelnuts, but here Michael makes it with peanuts. While Michael would probably cringe at this suggestion, if you're short on time, you can skip making the peanut butter powder from scratch and use a premade version like Just Great Stuff or PB2 (find it at most grocery stores). If you're making the powder from scratch, you can find maltodextrin at many specialty grocery stores or online.

Also, you can make the shells and the peanut butter powder in advance, even a month or two ahead of time. Store the powder at room temperature and the chocolate shells in the freezer, tightly wrapped (see Chef's Tips, page 60).

recipe continues on next page

Grown-Up Peanut Butter and Jelly Truffles continued

CHOCOLATE SHELLS

1 pound chocolate, 68 to 75 percent cocoa

PEANUT GIANDUJA

5 teaspoons cocoa butter

3 teaspoons couverture dark chocolate

⅓ cup peanut butter

6⅔ tablespoons hazelnut praline paste

PEANUT BUTTER POWDER

½ cup peanut butter

4 tablespoons tapioca maltodextrin (N-Zorbit) Maldon sea salt, for sprinkling on top

SPECIAL EQUIPMENT:

Plastic (not silicone) round truffle molds, pastry bag (for a DIY version, see Chef's Tips, page 60), paint scraper (yeah, like from a hardware store)

CHOCOLATE SHELLS

1. Line a couple of baking sheets with parchment paper. Then temper the chocolate, following the instructions on page 11.

2. Fill the truffle molds up to the top with the tempered chocolate. Using a fluid motion and keeping them horizontal to your kitchen counter, tap the molds against the edge of the counter to remove any air bubbles.

3. Flip the molds upside down onto the baking sheets and tap the backs of them with your hand or a spatula to encourage the excess chocolate to run out. The chocolate that remains in the mold will become your truffle shell.

4. Flip the molds right side up and tap on the counter again. Using some force, scrape across the horizontal surface of the molds with a clean paint scraper (or long offset spatula) to remove the excess chocolate spread across the molds.

5. Let the molds sit on the counter until cool, just a few minutes, then remove shells from molds. Lay a sheet of parchment paper on top of a large baking sheet. Firmly grasp the edges of the molds, and in one quick motion flip them upside down, so that the chocolate side rests on the parchment paper. Tap the molds forcefully; each shell should release naturally. Turn the shells right side up, then set aside.

PEANUT GIANDUJA

6. Heat the cocoa butter and chocolate in a small saucepan until melted. Add the peanut butter and praline paste, and heat the whole mixture to 113°F (45°C).

7. Remove the gianduja from the heat and stir with an offset spatula until the mixture cools to 86°F (30°C).

recipe continues on page 60

8. Transfer the gianduja to a pastry bag and fill the shells almost to the top, leaving room for peanut butter powder. Let rest in a cool room (70°F [21°C]) for an hour or in the refrigerator for 10 minutes.

PEANUT BUTTER POWDER

9. Spoon the peanut butter into the bowl of a food processor. With the processor running, slowly incorporate the tapioca maltodextrin until the mixture is a powdery consistency.

10. Spoon the powder into each gianduja-filled cup and sprinkle a few grains of Maldon salt on top. Enjoy!

CHEF'S TIPS

Buy pastry bags for recipes that call for piping ganache or dough, or make a DIY pastry bag with a gallon-size freezer bag. For either type of bag, place one bottom corner inside a large measuring cup or pitcher. Fold the top of the bag down over the edge of the cup. Spoon the ganache or dough into the bag until it fills the cup. Unfold the edges of the bag and lift the bag out of the cup. Push the ganache or dough all the way down. If you're using a pastry bag, use a twist tie or rubber band to close it; if you're using a freezer bag, seal it, and then use scissors to snip off a tiny piece of the corner, making an opening about ¼ inch across. Voilà!

Bonbons and truffles will last up to two weeks when stored at room temperature and up to six months when frozen (do not store them in the refrigerator). If you're storing them in the freezer, keep in mind that transitioning them into and out of the cold more slowly cuts down on condensation. Here's how to do it: Make sure the shells have completely hardened before placing them in a zip-lock freezer bag. Squeeze the air out of the bag and seal it, and then put it inside yet another bag, squeezing the air out of that one too. Refrigerate for 24 hours; then put in the freezer. When you're ready to unfreeze the shells, first defrost them in the fridge for 24 hours. Then take them out and let warm to room temperature before unwrapping them.

MADRE

All-American Tropical Chocolate

MADRE COFOUNDER NAT BLETTER calls making chocolate "applied ethnobotany." What the heck does the professor mean by that?

"If you start talking to someone in tongues, throwing the scientific names of plants at them, their eyes are going to glaze over," he explained. "But if you give them a bar of chocolate, maybe they'll remember it more."

That's especially true for Hawaiian cocoa, which will surprise anyone who thinks they know what chocolate tastes like. Think pineapple, watermelon, raisin. Hawaii is the only state in the United States where cacao can grow, and because it's an island ecosystem with varying weather systems, "you have all these pockets of different flavors," Nat explained.

Of course, cacao isn't native to Hawaii. Back in the 1850s German physician William Hillebrand brought it to the island and planted it in what's now the Foster Botanical Garden in Honolulu to see how it grew. However, no one attempted to make chocolate from Hawaiian-grown cacao for almost 100 years. Now it's a different story. Bean-to-bar makers have cropped up all over the islands, calling their chocolate "**tree to bar**." That means they take "bean to bar" one step further: they grow the cacao themselves as well as ferment, dry, roast, grind, and smoothen the cocoa into chocolate.

Madre Chocolate started out on a different path, though. After getting his PhD in ethnobotany, teaching at the University of Hawaii, and making chocolate at home, Nat decided to take the plunge. In 2010 he cofounded the company with friend and colleague David Elliott; because they were in Hawaii, the two decided to focus

continued on next page

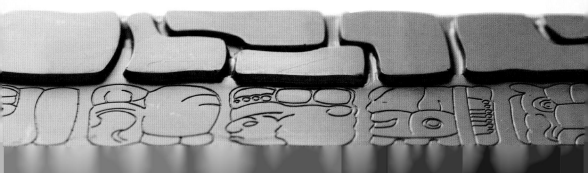

MADRE continued

on (duh) Hawaiian cocoa. They make amazing single-origin bars as well as bars with unusual inclusions like triple cacao (ground and refined beans with cacao fruit pulp and roasted nibs), many of which have won awards.

Nat and Dave have been buying much of Madre's cocoa from Hawaiian and Central American farmers. They wanted to perfect the chocolate-making process before they started growing plants and processing cacao. But now they're ready. They recently started growing cacao on their own farm, and they've been fermenting beans for farmers for a few years. Nat even calls Madre "the epicenter for cacao processing in Hawaii." "Understanding the ferment has really honed our craft," he said, "because it adds at least three-fourths of the flavor to the finished chocolate. The farmer should get most of the credit for the flavor of the chocolate, and most chocolate makers have been trying to take so much of the credit for what they do." After all, it's usually the farmer who ferments the beans.

So now, for the first time in history, one place is home to cacao farmers, chocolate makers, and a research university, the University of Hawaii, where specialists analyze everything from fermentation times to pest problems. That means that in Hawaii, they've been able to "close the design loop of cacao processing and create a rapid design cycle," Nat said. In other words, farmers can get feedback on their fermenting process immediately instead of having to wait a year or more (until the cocoa has been shipped to makers in other countries and turned into chocolate).

Madre is sharing its knowledge too. Nat and Dave have visited the Dominican Republic, the Solomon Islands, and Vanuatu to help farmers learn how to ferment cacao correctly and therefore be able to charge a better price (anywhere from two to four times as much) for their product. They're planning to do the same thing in the Philippines, Haiti, and Vietnam.

For Nat, "applied ethnobotany" means more than just cacao, though. Outside the Madre shop in Honolulu, he's planted a 2,000-square-foot garden where they grow almost every plant they use in their chocolate: sugarcane, vanilla, coffee, passion fruit, ginger. And they've just opened a café in the same location where they serve traditional Central American chocolate drinks like champurrado (see the recipe on page 75) and bu'pu (an Oaxacan beverage made with plumeria flowers). "We try to give cacao seeds and seedlings to everyone who comes to our shop who lives in Hawaii," Nat said. "We're calling ourselves Johnny Cacao Seed."

TYPES OF COCOA

GENETICS ISN'T JUST responsible for giving you your father's curly hair or your mother's crooked grin; they also play a huge part in the way chocolate looks, smells, and tastes. Genetics gets really nerdy really fast, and chocolate experts are still exploring the cacao genome and its history. But the reason it matters here is that some genetics-related terms show up on labels, and it's helpful to understand what the heck people are talking about.

For many years, people have divided cocoa into three groups: **Criollo**, **Forastero**, and **Trinitario**. Criollo (the name means "native") is thought to be the best in terms of flavor, but the cacao is finicky and hard to grow. Forastero ("foreign") is often said to be lacking in flavor but hardy. When people brought cacao from Central and South America to other continents as a cash crop, they almost exclusively brought Forastero because of its sturdy nature as well as the fact that Forastero produces more pods with many more seeds than Criollo. Criollo, on the other hand, is considered **fine-flavor cocoa** — the type of cocoa that craft makers want to use. So Forastero, and, by extension, most African-grown Forastero cocoa, gets left in the dust to be used by industrial chocolate makers like Mars. It's called **bulk cocoa**. Meanwhile, Trinitario (so named because it originated in Trinidad) is a

hybrid of Criollo and Forastero; though it has some Forastero in it, it's still considered fine-flavor cocoa.

If you start hanging out with chocolate nerds, you'll hear them talk about the superiority of some cocoa over others:

"Oh, I tasted an amazing Criollo the other day."

"Yeah? I bet it wasn't as good as this rare Criollo I found last year. All of the beans were white!"

"Shows what you know. That's not a Criollo. It's a Nacional variety that happens to have white beans."

"Whatever. At least it's not a Forastero. Who would want to eat that?"

It turns out it's much more complicated than the whole Criollo/Forastero/Trinitario trifecta. In 2008 a researcher named Juan Carlos Motamayor discovered 10 genetic families of cacao, which are named according to geographic origin: Amelonado, Contamaná, Criollo, Curaray, Guiana, Iquitos, Marañón, Nacional, Nanay, and Purús. (Notice that because Forastero is actually made up of several distinct genetic groups, it's not on this list.) Since then other researchers have identified 3 additional families and believe that there are somewhere around 20 to 25 distinct types. However, they haven't reconciled their findings with Motamayor's work or named the families, so for now we're sticking with the 10 names mentioned above. To make it extra confusing, beans within the same pod can have different genetics, meaning that the chocolate made from them is often a mishmash and rarely a true genetic match to any of these terms.

Before I get too scientific on you, here's what you really need to know. There are four main types of cocoa: Criollo, Forastero, Trinitario, and Nacional, which has been added to the original trifecta because of its distinct flavor profile. Everyone still clamors over Criollo, because it's known for its nuanced flavors. (In particular people prize **Porcelana** Criollo beans, which are delicate and easy to overroast. Unlike most cocoa, Porcelana beans are white, which creates a lighter-colored chocolate. Makes sense, since *porcelana* means "porcelain" in Spanish.) Nacional is highly valued for its distinct floral notes (think orange blossom and jasmine). Until recently it was thought to be specific to Ecuador, but in the past few years it has also been found in a valley in Peru (see page 118 for more info). Ecuadorian Nacional is also called Arriba.

Meanwhile, Forastero is a term that is still widely used but no longer botanically accurate, since, as it turns out, many different types of cocoa were lumped into that category. In this new age, the idea that they are all inferior has been thrown out the window. Askinosie Chocolate makes award-winning chocolate using Forastero beans from Tanzania, and French maker François Pralus turns out some amazingly flavorful bars from Tanzania, Ghana, and other places that technically produce bulk cocoa. In other words, not all Forastero is bad, even though it has that reputation.

Last but not least, the Trinitario classification is still accurate: it's a genetic hybrid of Criollo and any other genetic strain previously thought to be Forastero. Trinitario is also considered a fine-flavor cocoa.

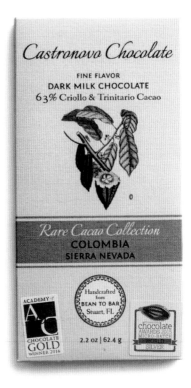

Castronovo uses a blend of Criollo and Trinitario cacao in this award-winning dark milk chocolate bar.

Hybrids

In addition to Trinitario, there are all sorts of other natural and man-made cacao hybrids. They usually have technical names with numbers in them. The worst of these are man-made hybrids like the dreaded **CCN-51**, a bean that yields almost four times the industry average and is disease-resistant but requires a ton of fertilizers and pesticides. According to Darin Sukha of the Cocoa Research Centre, "It has very dirty and undesirable flavor attributes that are different from what you find in fine-flavor cocoa and even bulk cocoa."

Here's everything you need to know about CCN-51.

- Companies that use it: Mars, Cadbury, Cargill Inc., Barry Callebaut, Blommer Chocolate
- Was introduced to Peru by the US Agency for International Development in 2002 to persuade farmers to grow another crop besides coca (which, as you probably know, is the base for cocaine)
- Accounted for 36 percent of cacao production in Ecuador in 2015
- Can spread quickly to other trees because (thanks to tiny midges) cacao plants cross-pollinate faster than you can say, "Pass the cookies."
- Chocolate experts and eaters almost everywhere describe it as, in a word, disgusting.

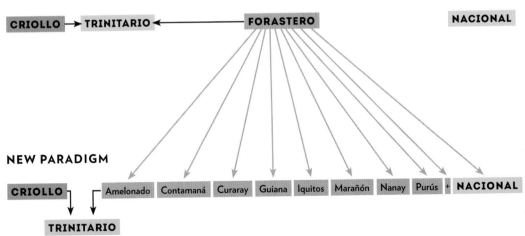

OLD PARADIGM

CRIOLLO → TRINITARIO ← FORASTERO   NACIONAL

NEW PARADIGM

CRIOLLO   Amelonado Contamaná Curaray Guiana Iquitos Marañón Nanay Purús + **NACIONAL**

TRINITARIO

High-End Cocoa

These days chocolate labels are getting fancier and fancier. Many of them name the exact origin of their beans. You may not immediately think of origin as a "type" of cocoa, but that's often how the beans are described in nerdy chocolate circles. Here are the most desirable types, with delicate, nuanced flavors that make them worth more money. Sometimes you'll also see the specific variety of cocoa on a label, so I've included that shortlist below as well.

ORIGIN

- Camino Verde, Ecuador
- Chuao, Venezuela
- Esmeraldas, Ecuador
- Marañón Canyon, Peru
- Ocumare, Venezuela
- Piura, Peru
- Príncipe
- Rio Caribe, Venezuela
- Sambirano Valley, Madagascar
- São Tomé
- Sur del Lago de Maracaibo, Venezuela
- Trinidad
- Xoconuzco, Mexico

VARIETY OF CACAO

- Beniano
- Nacional
- Porcelana

Then there's **heirloom cacao**, a special designation from the Fine Chocolate Industry Association's Heirloom Cacao Preservation Fund, assigned because of its genetic qualities and superior taste.

At the end of the day, when you start with a solid bean and factor in good processing and a skilled maker, well, you're in for some fantastic chocolate.

Single-Origin Brownie Flight

Recipe from Dandelion Chocolate
(read more about them on page 191!)

LEVEL:
Medium

Yield

24
very rich
brownies

THE FIRST TIME I visited Dandelion Chocolate's café in San Francisco, I almost OD'd on good chocolate. Imagine me with a mug of drinking chocolate, a cacao-fruit smoothie, three bars of chocolate, and a brownie flight.

What exactly is a brownie flight? Well, let me tell you. Among all of Dandelion's fantastic baked goods, this one takes the cake: three brownies on one plate, each made with a distinct single-origin chocolate. You can taste the flavor notes of each origin, whether it's a cherry-berry flavor in chocolate from Madagascar or a sense of smoke in chocolate from Papua New Guinea.

I highly recommend adding a flight to your next chocolate tasting party. Just make three batches of brownies, following this recipe, and using a different type of single-origin chocolate for each one. When you're ready to serve, put one brownie of each type on each plate. If you only have time to make one batch, you may not taste the flavor notes as distinctly as if you tried it against two other types, but you'll still be in for a delightful brownie.

2⅓ cups chopped single-origin chocolate (70 percent cocoa)

¾ cup (1½ sticks) butter, cubed

1⅓ cups sugar

3 eggs

1 teaspoon vanilla extract

1 cup plus 2 tablespoons all-purpose flour

Pinch of salt

recipe continues on next page

BROWNIE
BITE FLIGHT

The individual flavor
nuances of our single-origin
chocolate shine through even
in brownies. We've noted
what we taste but each
palate differs so explore and
look for your own, personal
notes too.

VENEZUELA
notes: chocolatey

PAPUA NEW GUINEA
notes: smoky, molasses

MADAGASCAR
notes: dried cherries

The brownie bite flight from Dandelion's San Francisco store

1. Preheat the oven to 325°F (163°C).
   Line an 8- by 12-inch sheet cake pan with
   parchment paper or a silicone mat.

2. Melt 1 cup chocolate and the butter in a
   double boiler or microwave (in short intervals), stirring occasionally.

3. Whisk together the sugar, eggs, and vanilla
   in a medium bowl. Then add the mixture to
   the melted chocolate and stir well.

4. Fold in the flour and salt.

5. Fold in the remaining 1⅓ cups chocolate.

6. Pour the mixture onto the prepared sheet
   cake pan, and use a rubber spatula to
   smooth it out evenly.

7. Bake for 14 to 16 minutes, turning the pan
   halfway through the baking time.

8. Let cool completely, then place the tray
   in the freezer for an hour or two, to help
   the brownies firm up so you can cut them
   neatly. Cut with a sharp knife into small
   pieces. Plate and enjoy!

THE AMERICAN WAY

AMERICANS WANT TO stand out, or so it seems. We pride ourselves on our individuality, our creativity, and our ability to innovate. As I mentioned in chapter 1, in the early 2000s, American makers weren't interested in creating chocolate from scratch in the traditional European style. They viewed the additions of cocoa butter and vanilla as adulterations of the pure ingredients, and they wanted to challenge themselves as well as to develop a new style of chocolate, an American style. That's why many of them focused on using only two ingredients: cocoa and sugar. Rather than following the European methods of balancing all the flavors to create an even, deep chocolate taste, offset with cocoa butter and vanilla, American makers started to exaggerate the natural flavor notes in each variety of cacao, so that you immediately tasted what that bean was about. The resulting chocolate was big, bold, and brash — like, well, Americans — and it's inspired a new school of bean-to-bar makers across the world.

For example, in 2013 Massachusetts-based Rogue Chocolatier revolutionized the prized Porcelana beans from Venezuela by using them to make a bar with very little sugar. Porcelana (a type of Criollo cacao) is known for its neutral and almost buttery flavors, with little acid or fruity notes and almost no astringency. But maker Colin Gasko's

80 percent bar surprises the heck out of those who expect Porcelana to be delicate and mild. Colin's is "punchier and more dynamic than I've ever tasted," Aubrey Lindley, who owns the specialty chocolate shop Cacao in Portland, Oregon, told me. When I tried the Rogue Porcelana bar, its bitter, harsh notes almost took over, but I could still taste

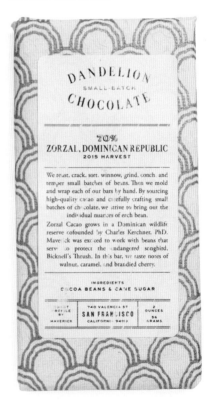

Like many American makers, Dandelion uses only two ingredients (cocoa beans and cane sugar) and focuses on flavor.

the peachiness underneath. Though it's not my favorite Porcelana, Colin certainly showcases what the beans can do, and makes a point. "I was trying to push boundaries and show what's possible in chocolate," he said. His was the first real American bar made with those particular beans (Scharffen Berger had a vanity project a while back but didn't even sell the chocolate); these days you'll find Porcelana from many makers — but not many 80 percent bars.

The pendulum is swinging back. American makers still want to exaggerate those natural flavor notes in the cocoa, but they are also starting to introduce cocoa butter into their bars, and some even use (gasp!) vanilla. For about a decade the "serious" makers made only single-origin bars, but now we're starting to see blends as well as **inclusions** (like sea salt or raspberries).

Some, like Dandelion Chocolate and Rogue Chocolatier, are sticking to their two-ingredient guns, but in general American makers have opened their arms (and mouths) to other ingredients. In some ways this is simple practicality, another American trademark. As many makers will tell you, people like to eat flavored bars. So they're making the most amazing flavored bars you've ever tasted.

Chocolate makers are getting creative with inclusions. An inclusion is an added ingredient that significantly alters the flavor and/or texture of the chocolate, such as almonds, sea salt, or dried raspberries. In other words, it's a fancy way of saying there's stuff in your chocolate.

THE MOST INTERESTING INGREDIENTS
in Craft Chocolate

AMARANTH

BLACK PEPPER

BLUE CHEESE

BREAD CRUMBS

BOURBON CASK–
AGED COCOA NIBS

CHILES

COCONUT MILK

COFFEE AND
CARDAMOM

GINGERBREAD

HORCHATA

JERK SPICES

MALTED MILK

POP ROCKS

QUINOA

ROSE PETALS

TEA

WINE

TAZA

Transforming a
Mexican Drink
into a Bar with Bite

THE ESKIMOS MAY HAVE 50 WORDS for snow, but I'd much rather be a Mayan, since they have lots of different words for chocolate, in all its many forms. My favorite is *chokola'j*: "to drink chocolate together."

Because for most of its life, chocolate has been a drink. In Central and South America, it was traditionally a savory, spicy, hot beverage mixed with corn, chiles, and all sorts of spices, then beaten until it was frothy and served to royalty. Europeans used to drink it alongside their tea and coffee too, while they talked philosophy and politics. But the idea of eating chocolate — well, that's new. Englishman Joseph Fry discovered how to make it into a solid back in 1847, and since then, we Americans have never looked back.

Except for Taza Chocolate, that is. Taza makes stone-ground eating chocolate in the Mexican tradition: In Mexico, most people still drink their chocolate. They grind it roughly with add-ins like sugar, almonds, and spices; mold it into tablets; and then drop the tablets into hot water and drink it down. "I was totally enamored by that idea," CEO and founder Alex

Whitmore told me. "That chocolate doesn't have to be this European traditional waxy smooth confection."

When he visited Mexico in the early 2000s, Alex "was blown away by these rudimentary stone mills used to grind roasted cocoa beans into fine liquor." The liquor was then mixed with sugar into something called *chocolate para mesa*, "chocolate for the table," he told me. Making it himself, though, wasn't that easy. The rotary stones are carved with intricate patterns that are the work of an individual mill worker, or *molinero*. And they'll be damned if they'll give away their trade secrets. If you try to apprentice with one of them, "they look at you like, 'Who is this?!' " Alex explained. Molineros traditionally pass the methods for "dressing" the stones (carving the patterns) from father to son (they're rarely women), and it's hard to penetrate that inner circle. In fact, when it's time to repair the stones, molineros will even take them off the mill and go somewhere private to fix them!

Why is it such a big deal? Each ingredient (cocoa, sugar, corn, and so on) needs a different stone with a different pattern, and one tiny error in the pattern can totally alter the result. "If we were to pass a sugared mass through the [chocolate] liquor *molinos*," Alex said, "it would fill the room with smoke, and the whole thing would caramelize."

Alex eventually convinced a molinero named Carlos to show him some basic techniques — for example, how to carve a flowerlike pattern into a flat stone using a hammer and chisel. But he learned almost everything he knows from books and trial and error. Eventually he found a process that works.

The result is an eating chocolate unlike anything else: earthy, grainy, flavorful. Taza altered the traditional recipe for an American audience so that we can eat the stuff in solid form, but you can still make a traditional chocolate drink by grating the chocolate and whisking it into hot milk or water. The bars are round, in the style of Mexican chocolate tablets. "We didn't want to hide behind a European form factor [of a rectangular bar]," Alex explained. "There are visual cues to signal that it might be different than a Hershey bar."

Because for Taza, the chocolate is important, but it's not everything. "The products we make are a call to action for the consumer," Alex said. He's hoping that the round chocolate bar with its grainy texture will start a discussion about our food systems — that people will think about not only how the food tastes but also where it comes from, who made it, and how it got here. That's why the company uses a direct-trade model and publishes exactly where they get

continued on next page

Taza's Alex Whitmore carving the stone wheel for a molino (left); fresh cacao beans being cut open (middle); a close-up of the interior of a molino (right)

TAZA continued

their beans and how much they pay farmers (read more about direct trade on page 166). "We're trying to lead the way and get other companies to step up their game so we can change the chocolate industry and the world in our own corner," Alex said.

So what happens when he brings some of his chocolate down to the farmers in Central and South America? "They'll eat our chocolate if I give them a piece," he said. "But they'll usually melt it down and make it into a drink."

Champurrado Drinking Chocolate

Recipe from Taza Chocolate

CORN MAY NOT BE the first ingredient that comes to mind when you think of hot chocolate, but indigenous Mesoamericans have been mixing it into their drinking chocolate for thousands of years. This type of blend is called *champurrado*, and you can still buy all sorts of variations of the beverage from vending tricycles on street corners in Mexico. Think of it like a hearty chocolate breakfast, somewhere closer to oatmeal than dessert. Oh, and be prepared to be full for hours.

This recipe comes from Taza Chocolate, and it calls for exactly half of a disk of their Mexican-style stone-ground chocolate. You can use any brand of chocolate that you want, as long as it's around 70 percent cocoa, but stone-ground works best (especially with added cinnamon). You can find masa harina (dried corn flour traditionally used to make tortillas) at most grocery stores or online; Bob's Red Mill brand is a good choice. If you can't find *piloncillo* (a block of unrefined cane sugar that tastes like smoky caramel), substitute palm sugar or coconut sugar but not brown sugar.

The ancient Mayans and Aztecs would froth their chocolate by pouring the drink from mug to mug, lifting their arms high up in the air to get a good distance between the mugs. In the sixteenth century, a tool called a **molinillo** came into fashion: it's essentially a wooden whisk that you rub between your palms; the cut corners of the wood agitate the liquid. If you want to be super authentic, pick one of these methods (and be prepared to get messy); otherwise a good old whisk will do.

recipe continues on page 77

KNOW THE DIFFERENCE

DRINKING CHOCOLATE
A thick, rich drink made of melted chocolate, sugar, and water, milk, or cream. Not to be confused with hot cocoa.

HOT COCOA
Alkalized cocoa powder mixed with hot milk or water. Often confused with drinking chocolate.

Champurrado Drinking Chocolate

continued

⅔ **ounce chocolate (70 percent cocoa or darker)**

1 **ounce piloncillo**

¾ **cup whole milk**

½ **cup water**

1 **tablespoon masa harina**

Pinch of salt

1. Finely grate the chocolate and piloncillo, keeping them separate. You should have about 2 tablespoons of each.

2. Whisk together the piloncillo, ½ cup of the milk, water, masa harina, and salt in a saucepan. Bring to a boil over medium heat, then reduce the heat and simmer, whisking often, until lightly thickened, about 3 minutes. Remove from the heat.

3. Add the chocolate and whisk until it is melted.

4. Vigorously whisk in the remaining ¼ cup milk to cool down the drink and create a nice frothy head. Enjoy!

CHAPTER THREE

TASTING *and* Eating

I HAVE TWO STASHES of chocolate in my house at all times: eating chocolates and tasting chocolates. "Eating chocolates" are bars and candies that I don't have to think about too hard. I can munch on them while I watch TV or, say, write a book about chocolate. Most of the time they're inclusion bars, like something with salt and almonds. "Tasting chocolates" are bars with more complexity that require my full attention. I taste these slowly, one square at a time, with no distractions. These are usually single-origin bars, where the maker has focused on highlighting the terroir of a specific bean. (I also have "baking chocolate" and "research chocolate," but all of them — and how they've taken over the entire kitchen — are a sore point in my household.) To me, the best chocolate bars are those that fit in both categories. They're something I can slow down and savor or enjoy without the intellectual backdrop, depending on the day and my mood.

A Quick and Dirty Guide to
TASTING CHOCOLATE

NO MATTER YOUR personal preferences, when you have a fine bar of chocolate in front of you, you don't want to be all Augustus Gloop about it. Take it slow, one smallish bite at a time. Here are some tips for tasting chocolate with all the care it deserves.

1. **WAKE AND TASTE**. The best time to taste is in the morning, when your palate has had its beauty sleep. Start with a plain old chocolate bar that doesn't include any add-ins like almonds or salt. Let your bar warm to room temperature before you even think about eating it, then break off one to three squares and listen for a sharp **snap** (a mark of quality chocolate). When you're tasting more than one bar at the same time, some people say to try them in order from the highest cocoa percentage to the lowest, while others prefer tasting from the lowest cocoa

MEXICO

MADAGASCAR

TANZANIA

percentage to the highest. Test both ways and see which you prefer.

2. **TAKE A LOOK**. Chocolate isn't just brown. The color of the bar will tell you a lot about the way it tastes. First off, are there white patches? That could be bloom, when the fat separates from the cocoa, and indicates that the texture is probably off. If there aren't any obvious defects, look more closely at the color. Chocolate from Ghana and Tanzania will be darker than chocolate from Madagascar, which is reddish. As we learned in chapter 2, some of the best cocoa beans in the world are white (Porcelana and Peruvian Nacional, if you want to get nerdy about names), which creates a lighter-colored chocolate. And if it's milk chocolate, it will, of course, be even lighter.

3. **STOP AND SMELL THE CHOCOLATE**. Who needs roses when you have cocoa beans and sugar? Smelling the chocolate before popping it in your mouth will help you figure out how it's going to taste. Does it smell sweet? Like vanilla? Like burnt rubber? The chocolate won't always taste the way it smells, but scent can reveal quite a lot about what's going on in that little brown bar.

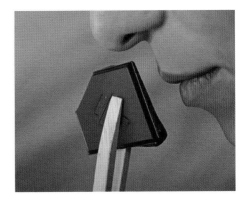

There are a lot of theories about how to best smell chocolate. Eagranie Yuh, author of *The Chocolate Tasting Kit*, says to "hold the chocolate between your thumb and index finger, cup your other hand around it like you're going to tell it a secret, bring it to your nose, and smell it." Others say to place the chocolate on a plate or a piece of paper before smelling it, since any smells on your fingers might mask what's going on in the chocolate. Regardless of the method you use, bring the chocolate as close to your nose as possible and sniff deeply (pro tip: the edge of the chocolate that's just been cut or snapped often smells the strongest). Some people are super serious about the smelling portion of tasting chocolate, and at chocolate competitions you'll often see judges walking around with brown smudges on their noses.

4. **BITE OFF A PIECE.** Some people chew the chocolate completely, while others let it slowly melt on their tongue. I like to chew it once or twice and then stop. I close my eyes, let the chocolate melt on my tongue, and see what I taste.

Raisins? Sure. Red berries? Often. Walnut notes? You better believe it. Of course, you also might not taste anything but chocolatechocolate-chocolate. Try comparing that one bar to other bars and then see if you notice a difference. Chocolate expert Clay Gordon recommends trying four bars at a time and comparing and contrasting pairs to determine your favorite of the group (he calls this a "tasting pyramid"). A comparison tasting will definitely make it easier to pick out the specific flavors of each bar: one might be spicier than another or earthier. Use the flavor wheel (opposite) to help guide you.

Don't be distracted by texture. A smooth **mouthfeel** can, of course, intensify the experience of the chocolate, but texture isn't the same as taste. Grittier chocolates often have flavor profiles that are as complex as — if not more so — those of smooth chocolates.

Don't pummel your mouth with one chocolate right after the other. Slow down and use a palate cleanser like lemon water, plain crackers, or slices of green apple between bars. At the International Chocolate Awards, we judges use plain cold polenta. It doesn't taste great, but it works like a dream.

When you get really good like expert Ed Seguine, who has worked for Mars and Guittard and now owns his own company, you'll be able to taste different notes at the beginning, middle, and end of a piece of chocolate, like a wine's nose, body, and finish. These qualities are more detectable in some chocolates than in others; some have flavor notes that evolve as you eat them, while others stay more constant.

5. **TAKE NOTES.** The best tasters take vigilant notes, so they can remember what the heck they tasted the week before, as well as the disappointments and highlights. Many serious tasters won't characterize chocolate bars by which ones they liked or didn't like. Instead they'll break it down into aroma, sweetness, bitterness, acidity, roast, and so on, withholding

Snap!

Use your ears, too. The snap is the sharp sound a properly tempered chocolate bar makes when it's broken into two pieces. Experts look for a good snap as a mark of quality chocolate.

judgment on whether a chocolate is "good" or "bad." If you're planning to judge the International Chocolate Awards or the Good Food Awards, sure, go ahead with this strategy. If you're looking to find a few bars to enjoy, though, it's fine to note whether you liked it or didn't like it, and if you'd buy it again. After all, chocolate is about pleasure and fun.

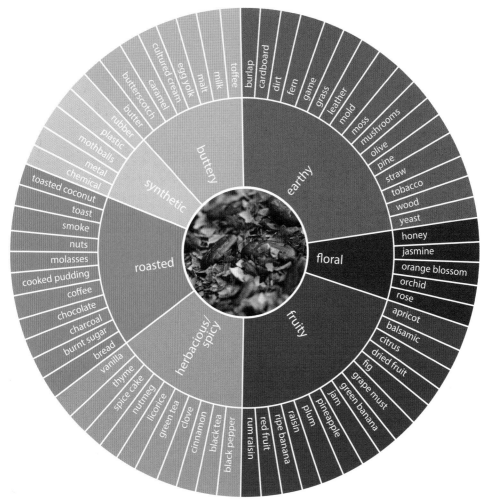

Here are all the flavors you might find in chocolate, in one tasty wheel.

AMANO

Chocolate Comes from Chocolate

ALMOST ALL CHOCOLATE MAKERS make chocolate because someone said they couldn't do it. That's certainly the case for Art Pollard, the force behind Amano Artisan Chocolate. While working for the Brigham Young University physics department as a student in the early 1990s, Art found himself chewing on a chocolate bar and mulling over how to make it himself.

"At that time chocolate was a mysterious ingredient," the soft-spoken 40-something told me. "Where does chocolate come from? Well, chocolate comes from chocolate." When he voiced his interest to coworkers, they scoffed, saying it was too hard, almost impossible, since only giant corporations made chocolate, not small companies, let alone individual people. And so the cacao seed was planted.

Nowadays you can buy good cocoa beans online, but back then it was almost as impossible to find beans as it was to figure out what to do with them. Art spotted some beans at a Mexican grocery store but quickly realized they were, in his words, "terrible." So he started looking for other ways to get his hands on good beans. The best way? Go get them himself.

This is still true today: the most dedicated makers visit farms personally, and Art was one of the first to do it. "If [the cocoa] is coming from a warehouse on the East Coast, you're missing half the story," Art explained. "But if you bought most of the farmer's annual production and you see that he put all this sweat and tears into it, then you want to honor the farmer by doing the best that you can." His first trip was in 2005 to Villahermosa, Mexico; he'd bought some rare white beans over the phone and traveled south to claim them in person. Since then he's drunk champurrado with Mayan descendants, navigated harrowing switchbacks on a cliff-side highway in Venezuela, and sampled cacao all the world over. He's been to Mexico, Ecuador, the Dominican Republic, Peru, Papua New Guinea, Samoa, and, most notably, Venezuela, where he found beans that yielded scrumptious bars with high-end cocoa you'd be hard-pressed to find from other American makers.

"I want people to swear when they eat my chocolate," he said. He calls it the "holy crap factor" — that you should be so delighted by the great taste when you eat a piece that you scream out, "Holy crap!" (or, you know, some other four-letter word). Art doesn't subscribe to the popular two-ingredient ethos of cocoa and sugar that you'll find among most American makers, saying that attitude is all about ego. Instead he uses cocoa butter and even vanilla to craft smooth, decadent chocolate that showcases the high quality of the beans and his skill as a craftsman.

Like many American makers, though, Art stuck to single-origin chocolates until 2015,

continued on next page

Art Pollard carefully cuts off a cacao pod from a high branch at a plantation in the Dominican Republic.

A M A N O continued

when he launched a line of inclusion bars: raspberry and rose, cardamom and black pepper, and mango and chile. The raspberry-rose bar in particular is based on a pastry that Art tried at Pierre Hermé in Paris — one that, when he took a bite, made him scream, "Holy crap!" Within a few months of its release, the chocolate had already won a silver medal at the prestigious International Chocolate Awards. It joins an impressive club. Art's bars consistently win prizes from the International Chocolate Awards, the London Academy of Chocolate, the San Francisco International Chocolate Salon, the Good Food Awards, and more.

That success hasn't gone to his head, though. He's still the humble, quiet person he's always been. And he still spends a good deal of his time visiting farmers across the world in search of the best cacao. On one trip to Venezuela, he brought his bars to farmers in Cuyagua. It was the first time they'd tasted chocolate made from the cacao they'd grown themselves. One of them took a thoughtful bite, then said, "This chocolate is like a river. The flavor takes me to all of these wild and wondrous places."

Art refurbished a vintage winnowing machine from the 1920s or 1930s.

Mayan Chocolate Mousse

Recipe from Lauren Adler, chief chocophile, and the Chocolopolis team

LEVEL: *Medium*

Serves

6

AUREN ADLER, the owner of specialty store Chocolopolis in Seattle, traveled with Taza Chocolate to Belize a few years ago, where she hung out with Mayan cacao farmers and "communed with howler monkeys in the jungles." One of the highlights of the trip? Watching the local farm wives make drinking chocolate from cocoa they'd fermented and dried themselves. They roasted and ground it with *Theobroma bicolor* (a relative of cacao) and allspice, then added hot water to the paste and drank the unsweetened beverage in calabash gourds. They told her that when a pregnant woman is going into labor, they add black pepper to the drink and serve it to her.

Lauren used that drink as inspiration, melding Mayan and European traditions to create an allspice-infused mousse.

She recommends using chocolate made with cocoa from Belize (especially Taza's single-origin bar), though any fruity chocolate will work.

A word to the wise: Don't crush the allspice berries. Crushing them can result in a rubbery chocolate-cream emulsion, whereas keeping them whole ensures a silky texture. One more tip: Start early. You'll want to prepare the mousse at least 6 hours before you plan to serve it, to give the flavors time to develop and to let the texture set up properly. If you have extra time, cover it and let it sit in the refrigerator overnight.

Oh, and by the way, don't wait until you're going into labor to enjoy this one. It's a glorious affair for all, gals and guys alike.

recipe continues on page 89

Mayan Chocolate Mousse
continued

MOUSSE

- ⅔ cup heavy whipping cream
- 1½ teaspoons whole allspice berries
- 4 tablespoons cultured butter (preferably 84 percent butterfat), softened
- 4½ ounces dark chocolate (70 to 77 percent cocoa), chopped
- 5 eggs
- 3 tablespoons ultrafine sugar

WHIPPED CREAM

- 1 cup heavy whipping cream, very cold
- 1 tablespoon granulated sugar
- ½ teaspoon vanilla extract
  Ground allspice or black pepper, for garnish

SPECIAL EQUIPMENT
Six 4-ounce ramekins, hand mixer or stand mixer

1. To make the mousse, combine the cream and allspice berries in a small saucepan and warm over low heat until the cream around the edge of the saucepan begins to boil. Immediately remove the pan from the heat. Cover the top of the pan tightly with plastic wrap to hold in the flavorful vapors of the allspice. Set aside for 30 minutes to let the flavors infuse. Then remove the plastic wrap and fish out the allspice berries.

2. Combine the butter and chocolate in a medium bowl and microwave at high power for 30 seconds. Check to see if they have melted. If not, microwave in intervals of 10 seconds until they are melted.

3. Add the cream to the melted chocolate and mix well.

4. Separate the eggs into yolks and whites. Set the whites in the refrigerator to keep them chilled. Whip the egg yolks into the chocolate and cream mixture until they're just incorporated.

5. With a hand mixer or in a stand mixer, beat the egg whites until soft peaks form. Add the ultrafine sugar and continue to beat until stiff peaks form.

6. Gently fold one-quarter of the egg whites into the chocolate mixture. Then fold in the remaining egg whites.

7. Dish the mousse into six ramekins, cover with plastic wrap, and place in the refrigerator to chill for at least 6 hours but preferably overnight.

8. Immediately before serving, make the whipped cream: Combine the whipping cream with the sugar and vanilla in a bowl. With a hand mixer or in a stand mixer, beat at high speed until soft peaks form. Be careful not to overwhip or you'll end up with a butterlike consistency.

9. Spoon or pipe the whipped cream on top of the ramekins. Garnish with a sprinkle of allspice or black pepper.

How to
PAIR CHOCOLATE

OME HERE, I have something to tell you. Closer . . . closer . . . ready? WINE ALMOST NEVER PAIRS WELL WITH CHOCOLATE.

Whew, I said it. I'm not the only one, though. Talk to almost any chocolate or wine expert and they will wax scientific about why this pairing doesn't work, with words like *tannins, polyphenols,* and so on. Matt Caputo, president of A Priori Specialty Foods (which distributes a lot of bean-to-bar chocolate) and Caputo's Market and Deli, says that pairing a big red with dark chocolate is like "shooting yourself in the tongue with Novocain." It's a strong sensation that will shock you into being awake, but it will also immediately give you palate fatigue and prevent you from tasting any of the nuances of the wine or the chocolate. Meanwhile, Michael Klug, a chocolatier at L. A. Burdick in New York City, who has been pairing chocolate with other foods for decades, is more mild-mannered about it. "Dark chocolate is so powerful that it covers the subtle flavors and finesse that is found in wine instead of highlighting it. The matching of fine high-end dry red wines and also white wines and Champagne is a very unfortunate combination."

Unfortunate indeed. That's why I'm taking a step away from the classic wine-chocolate pairing and toward some more unusual pairings. Think cheese, bread, and mezcal. I'm also including some ideas for sweet wines with chocolate, since these are easier to match. I put together a panel of expert

tasters — chocolatiers, cicerones, sommeliers, coffee experts, tea experts, and other people with great palates — to test through the following combinations, and I'm excited to share the results with you.

For the chocolate, you'll see overriding flavor notes instead of origins, because one Madagascar bar, for example, might taste different from another, and because blends will work just as well as single origins for these pairings. We used 70 percent cocoa — that is, dark chocolate — as our go-to percentage, but we also tried milk chocolate (which was usually about 40 percent), dark milk chocolate (55 to 70 percent, give or take a few), **100 percent bars**, and white chocolate. Keep in mind that the percentage, roast style (light or dark), and overall chocolate style (two-ingredient or added cocoa butter, for example) will change pairings significantly. In other words, trust your own taste buds!

Remember, these are just suggestions. At the end of the day, you are your own best chocolate sommelier. Have fun with it, and don't be afraid to mix and match to find a pairing that you like. Here are some basic guidelines:

- Pair foods with similar flavors. For example, a nutty chocolate can bring out the hazelnut taste in an already nutty cheese.
- Or pair foods with opposite flavors. If the above example was nuts on nuts, now think peanut butter and jelly.

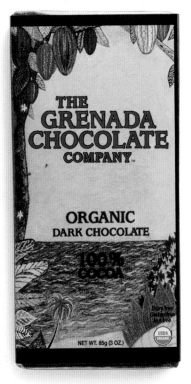

A 100 percent bar is a chocolate bar made with only one ingredient: cocoa beans. That means there's not even any sugar in it! Some might call it bitter and unpalatable, others the true essence of chocolate.

- Use the aromatics of the chocolate or the other ingredients to guide you.
- Consider whether the pairing makes each element taste better or worse. If better, awesome: you've found a winner. If worse, move on to the next one.
- Trial and error is your best friend. Worst-case scenario? You get to eat a lot of chocolate!

The best pairings will taste like a third food, not simply a mashup of chocolate with cheese in your mouth, for example. They'll create another experience altogether, one that surprises and delights — and keeps you coming back for more.

Now to the pairings!

BEVERAGE PAIRINGS

FOR ALL BEVERAGE PAIRINGS, I recommend a modified version of what Murray's Cheese in New York calls the "milk-shake method." Murray's uses the method for tasting cheese with a second food or beverage, whereas we're using it to taste chocolate with a second food or beverage. Here's how it works: Take a bite of the chocolate, chew it a couple of times, then let it start to melt in your mouth. Then take a sip of the beverage and let the flavors meld. (If it's tea or coffee, slurp as you sip to aerate the drink.) Now try it in reverse: with just a hint of the liquid still in your mouth, take a bite of chocolate and see what you taste.

Chocolate and Tea

Aromatics. If I could describe tea in one word, that would be it. That makes tea ideal to pair with chocolate, which can smell and taste like so many different things. The aromatics in tea tend to intensify the taste of the chocolate, highlighting flavors that are similar in both or contrasting opposing flavors so you can taste each even better. When I taste-tested them together, I found that the chocolate often intensified the tea, bringing out its natural sweetness, nuttiness, or toastiness in particular. Here are a few other insights from the tasting panel on the tea-chocolate combination:

- "Umami"
- "Like grilled fruit"
- "Rum raisin"
- "When you've roasted red peppers in the oven and you're removing the skin"
- "Super orangey"
- "Like Tibetan butter tea"

Pair chocolate with warm but not super-hot tea. You could try this with iced tea as well, but it would need to be closer to lukewarm than iced, since chocolate will not melt in your mouth the same way if your mouth is cold.

One thing you should know is that there are five families of tea (pictured on page 94), and within them certain flavor notes work particularly well with chocolate. Also note that any tea in any category can be fruit flavored; pair fruit-flavored teas with chocolates that have those same flavor notes (for example, citrus with citrus, berry with berry, and so on) or with chocolates that have contrasting flavor notes (for example, fruity with earthy, floral with nutty, and so on).

CHOCOLATE & TEA PAIRINGS

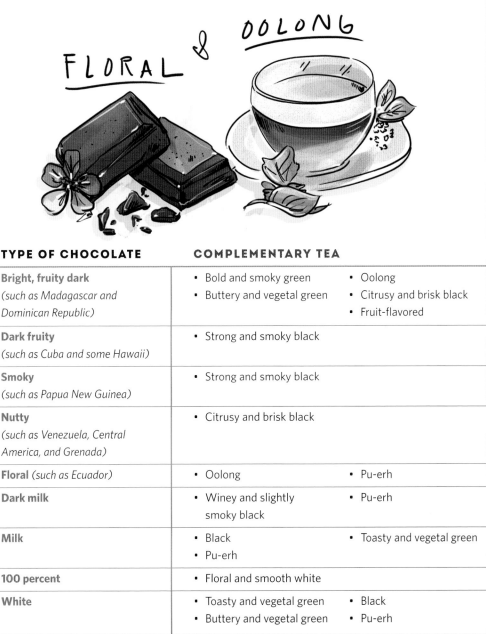

FLORAL & OOLONG

TYPE OF CHOCOLATE	COMPLEMENTARY TEA	
Bright, fruity dark *(such as Madagascar and Dominican Republic)*	• Bold and smoky green • Buttery and vegetal green	• Oolong • Citrusy and brisk black • Fruit-flavored
Dark fruity *(such as Cuba and some Hawaii)*	• Strong and smoky black	
Smoky *(such as Papua New Guinea)*	• Strong and smoky black	
Nutty *(such as Venezuela, Central America, and Grenada)*	• Citrusy and brisk black	
Floral *(such as Ecuador)*	• Oolong	• Pu-erh
Dark milk	• Winey and slightly smoky black	• Pu-erh
Milk	• Black • Pu-erh	• Toasty and vegetal green
100 percent	• Floral and smooth white	
White	• Toasty and vegetal green • Buttery and vegetal green	• Black • Pu-erh

Here are the tea families and their flavor notes:

BLACK TEA
- Citrusy and brisk (Ceylon)
- Strong and smoky (Lapsang souchong)
- Winey and slightly smoky (Keemun)

GREEN TEA
- Bold and smoky (gunpowder green)
- Buttery and vegetal (matcha)
- Toasty and vegetal (genmaicha)

WHITE TEA
- Floral and smooth (white peony)

OOLONG TEA
- Honey notes (Nepalese or Chinese)

PU-ERH
- Earthy

Chocolate and Coffee

Two types of beans, so many similarities. Both grow in tropical areas ranging from roughly 20 degrees above to 20 degrees below the equator; both require similar processes for growing, drying, and turning them into chocolate bars and coffee drinks; and both contain crazy flavor notes, from nutty to fruity to mushroomy. You'll find them paired together in mocha drinks, chocolate bars, and, if you're lucky, a square of chocolate on your plate after a shot of espresso. But not many people have dared to pair the two roasty beans together in quite this way.

But quite a few chocolate-coffee pairings actually work! With the help of my tasting panel, I grouped coffees into four loose categories: three origins and one type (espresso). Keep in mind that the exact characteristics I list below aren't always present in all coffees from these countries; like with chocolate, flavors can vary based on a number of factors. But here are some guiding principles:

- **Nutty coffees** (Colombia and other South American origins)
- **Fruity and earthy coffees** (Central American origins)
- **Fruity and bright coffees** (Ethiopian, Rwandan, and Kenyan)
- **Espresso shots**

These pairings work best with unflavored black coffee. Skip the hazelnut and vanilla varieties as well as the sugar, since they can mask the flavors and sweetness of the chocolate. But if you like milk or cream in your coffee, go right ahead. It may mute the flavors of the chocolate and coffee a bit, but the pairings should still work. That goes for

CHOCOLATE & COFFEE PAIRINGS

NUTTY & NUTTY

TYPE OF CHOCOLATE	COMPLEMENTARY COFFEE
Bright, fruity dark *(such as Madagascar and Dominican Republic)*	• Nutty • Fruity and earthy • Fruity and bright
Dark Fruit *(such as Cuba and some Hawaii)*	• Fruity and earthy • Fruity and bright
Earthy *(such as Tanzania and Philippines)*	• Nutty • Fruity and earthy • Fruity and bright
Nutty *(such as Venezuela, Central America, and Grenada)*	• Nutty • Fruity and earthy • Fruity and bright
Floral *(such as Ecuador)*	• Fruity and earthy • Fruity and bright
Dark Milk	• Espresso shots
Milk	• Nutty • Fruity and earthy • Fruity and bright

espresso drinks like cappuccinos and lattes too, but keep in mind that you'll want to match these milk-based drinks with darker chocolates. As Counter Culture's Matt Banbury (an integral member of the tasting panel!) told me, "If you use a truly roasty coffee, it will become more toastlike in a milk-based drink. If you use something with a raw sugar sweetness, it may become more caramel." Sounds delicious to me.

Similarly, milk chocolate is a natural pairing for black coffee. As chocolate expert Eagranie Yuh says in *The Chocolate Tasting Kit*, "Its creaminess mellow[s] the coffee's acidity and slight bitterness." She recommends matching cappuccinos with high-percentage dark chocolates and avoiding highly acidic coffees, which tend to make chocolate taste sour.

As you do with tea, taste chocolate with warm but not super-hot coffee, using the milk-shake method outlined on page 92. One exception, though: you'll want to drink straight-up espresso shots first, swallow, then taste the chocolate. Otherwise the espresso could overwhelm the flavors of the chocolate.

Here are a few of my favorite notes from the tasting panel:

- "Like wearing the right polka dots and plaids together"
- "A wall of sound"

- "There's a certain salinity that adds a through line"
- "Fruity contrast"
- "Brings out the milk chocolatyness of it"

Chocolate and Beer

You've already forgotten about chocolate and red wine, right? Good, because chocolate and beer is a much better pairing. I know, it sounds crazy! But try it; it works. Something about the yeast and hops in the beer plays with the flavors of chocolate, creating a sublime experience that you'll want to re-create again and again. You'll want to pair like with like here — in other words, chocolate with citrusy notes against beer with citrusy notes, and chocolate with roasty notes against beer with roasty notes. Though an ice-cold beer sometimes hits the spot, it won't work when you're pairing it with chocolate. Make sure your beer is slightly warmer than you'd usually serve it (above 50°F [10°C]); otherwise the chocolate won't melt in your mouth so luxuriously.

There are so many types of beer that I can't even keep track, but a few work particularly well with chocolate:

- **IPAs** (American)
- **Ales** (Belgian, English brown, sours)
- **Stouts and porters** (milk stouts, dry Irish stouts, American porters)

CHOCOLATE & BEER PAIRINGS

STOUT

MILK & CHOCOLATE

TYPE OF CHOCOLATE	COMPLEMENTARY BEER
Bright, Fruity Dark (such as Madagascar and Dominican Republic)	• Stouts and porters • IPAs • Ales
Earthy (such as Tanzania and Philippines)	• IPAs
Nutty (such as Venezuela, Central America, and Grenada)	• Stouts and porters • Ales
Floral (such as Ecuador)	• Ales
Dark Milk	• Stouts and porters
Milk	• Stouts and porters

The Belgian ale reigned supreme when pairing with chocolate. Think Belgian blondes, Belgian golden strong ales, Belgian dubbels, Belgian dark strong ales, and the catchall Belgian Grand Cru category. And with their chocolaty, creamy consistencies, stouts and porters make a natural choice for chocolate. But don't overlook unlikely beers like citrusy IPAs, which can either bring out those flavors in an already fruity chocolate or complement an earthy one like nobody's business.

Chocolate and Spirits

Look at you, with your sipping whiskey and your cigar, lounging in your vintage Eames leather chair, calling to your live-in chef to bring you a delicious dessert to accompany your luxuries. Oh wait, that was a daydream. But here's a way to make your next sip of a spirit feel that sumptuous: pair it with a piece (or two or three) of craft chocolate.

As with beer, you'll want to pair like with like: floral spirits like gin with floral chocolates like single-origin Ecuador, and so on. You'll find some surprises when you try these together, as chocolate often brings out new flavors in the spirits and sometimes even transposes its flavors onto a spirit.

Also, though you might usually order some of these spirits on the rocks, keep it neat when you're pairing them with chocolate, as a cooler-temperature drink will change the way the chocolate melts in your mouth.

Many craft makers have started to age nibs in whiskey and bourbon barrels to infuse their bars with flavors. So it's no surprise that chocolate goes so well with the strong stuff. But it's not just whiskey, bourbon, and rye that work. Here are six types of spirits that pair particularly well:

- Gin
- Dry curaçao
- Tequila
- Mezcal
- Rum
- Whiskey, bourbon, rye, and Scotch

Chocolate and Fortified Wines

This one is easy. Sweet wines like sherry, port, and Madeira, as well as digestifs like amaro, pair well with dark, milk, white, and 100 percent chocolate. The higher sugar and the lower alcohol contents make them work, creating a sublime experience. You can even try regular old sweet wines like ice wines and some Rieslings. **ONE RULE: The wine must be sweeter than the chocolate.** I'm not going to divvy up wines and chocolates here, since most pair so well. Instead I'll simply say, have at it!

CHOCOLATE & SPIRITS PAIRINGS

WHITE & TEQUILA

TYPE OF CHOCOLATE	COMPLEMENTARY SPIRITS		
Slightly Fruity Dark (*such as mellower Madagascar and Dominican Republic*)	• Dry curaçao	• Mezcal	
Very Fruity Dark (*such as bright, acidic Madagascar and Dominican Republic*)	• Whiskey • Rye	• Bourbon • Scotch	
Smoky (*such as Papua New Guinea*)	• Mezcal	• Scotch	
Earthy (*such as Tanzania and Philippines*)	• Gin	• Mezcal	
Nutty (*such as Venezuela, Central America, and Grenada*)	• Whiskey • Rye	• Bourbon • Scotch	
Floral (*such as Ecuador*)	• Tequila		
Dark Milk	• Dry curaçao		
Milk	• Dry curaçao	• Gin	• Rum
White	• Gin	• Tequila	• Rum
Coffee Inclusions	• Whiskey • Rye	• Bourbon • Scotch	
100 Percent	• Tequila		

Ceylon Tea Fudge Sauce

Adapted from **Earl Grey Fudge Sauce** in the
Momofuku Milk Bar cookbook, by Christina Tosi

LEVEL: *Medium*

Serves
2–4

CHOCOLATE AND TEA go together like Beyoncé and Jay Z: great on their own, unstoppable together. That's why I love this recipe, which uses a tea that pairs well with chocolate to make a delicious fudge sauce with a twist. I based the recipe on one from Christina Tosi, one of my favorite pastry chefs and the amazing force behind Momofuku Milk Bar in New York City.

This fudge sauce has a strong tea flavor, so it isn't strictly necessary to use a single-origin chocolate, as unique flavors will be hidden behind the taste of the tea. If you do, I'd go with something mild and very chocolaty, like Venezuela, but a blend will work just as well. Pour this on top of the next sundae you make and you'll never go back to that stuff in a bottle again.

1 tablespoon Ceylon tea
   Pinch of ground cinnamon
¼ cup heavy cream, plus a few tablespoons extra
2 tablespoons unsweetened natural cocoa powder
2 tablespoons sugar
   Pinch of salt
1 ounce chocolate (65 to 70 percent cocoa), chopped
¼ cup glucose syrup

1. Combine the tea and cinnamon in a heatproof bowl.

2. Heat the ¼ cup of heavy cream in a saucepan just to boiling.

3. Pour the hot cream over the tea and cinnamon and let infuse for 5 minutes.

4. Strain the cream into a measuring cup. Add enough fresh heavy cream to bring the volume back up to ¼ cup.

5. Pour the cream back into the saucepan and warm over medium heat. Add the cocoa powder, sugar, and salt, and whisk until thoroughly combined.

6. Combine the chopped chocolate and glucose syrup in a bowl. Pour in the warm cream mixture and let sit for 1 minute to soften.

7. Using a spatula, start slowly stirring the sauce from the center in concentric circles, speeding up as it starts to get shinier and shinier, until it achieves a fudge sauce consistency, about 2 to 4 minutes.

8. Pour over ice cream, brownies, or whatever you desire, and enjoy! The sauce will keep in the fridge for up to 2 weeks in an airtight container. Do not freeze.

FOOD PAIRINGS

WHEN TASTING FOODS and chocolate together, you can use the milk-shake method again: First, put a small piece of the chocolate in your mouth, chew a couple of times, and let it start to melt. Then add the cheese, bread, or other food and chew slowly. Here are some tips for pairings with fruit, cheese, and bread.

Chocolate and Fruit

Chocolate is practically bursting with fruit flavors, from red berries to bright pineapple, and so it makes perfect sense to pair it with the real stuff. I particularly like to use these pairings to remind myself what each fruit tastes like, so I can better recognize fruity notes when tasting chocolate by itself, for judging or just for fun.

There are two ways to pair chocolate and fruit. I won't break these out into individual categories since you'll probably get the picture quickly.

PAIR LIKE FLAVORS TOGETHER. A Madagascar bar with bright blackberry notes gets paired with actual juicy blackberries, and a Hawaiian bar with distinct raisin notes goes with actual raisins. Be sure to clear your palate between each bite. You're trying to taste the similarities in each element, not necessarily combine them into one mishmash in your mouth.

PAIR OPPOSITE FLAVORS TOGETHER. A Venezuela bar with nutty notes goes with a tart fresh strawberry, and a Tanzania bar with earthy notes goes with fresh citrus. This is more of a true pairing experience, where you're trying both elements together and tasting the way they mingle in your mouth.

Chocolate and Cheese

I have an idea. Let's take two decadent foods and put them together for over-the-top decadence. Sound good? I thought so.

We aren't the only ones to think so, either. In the nineteenth century in Venezuela, it was common for people to eat something salty like cheese with chocolate for an afternoon snack. In *The New Taste of Chocolate*, Maricel Presilla says that when she's traveling in Colombia, she sees people eating chocolate with cheese *arepas* (thick cornmeal patties), and in the Colombian Andes, people still dunk Edam and Gouda in their drinking chocolate. It's time for us to get in on that goodness.

I've suggested some chocolate pairings below for a range of cheese families. Families of cheese? Yep, experts like to group them together as shown on page 104.

CHOCOLATE & CHEESE PAIRINGS

BLUE & SMOKY

TYPE OF CHOCOLATE	COMPLEMENTARY CHEESE	
Bright, Fruity Dark (such as Madagascar and Dominican Republic)	• Pressed and uncooked • Fresh	• Washed rind • Bloomy
Dark Fruit (such as Cuba and some Hawaii)	• Washed rind	• Blue
Smoky (such as Papua New Guinea)	• Fresh • Pressed and uncooked	• Washed rind • Blue
Earthy (such as Tanzania and Philippines)	• Pressed and uncooked	• Bloomy
Nutty (such as Venezuela, Central America, and Grenada)	• Pressed and uncooked	• Washed rind
Floral (such as Ecuador)	• Pressed and uncooked	
Dark Milk	• Washed rind • Pressed and uncooked	• Pressed and cooked • Blue
Milk	• Washed rind	• Pressed and cooked
Coffee Inclusions	• Washed rind	• Blue
Almond Inclusions	• Pressed and uncooked	
100 Percent	• Sweet blues (like Rogue Creamery Smokey Blue)	

CHEESE FAMILIES

FRESH
- Chèvre
- Mozzarella
- Burrata

BLOOMY
- Double-crème French Brie
- Fromager d'Affinois

WASHED RIND
- Taleggio
- Epoisses

PRESSED AND COOKED
- Parmigiano Reggiano
- Challerhocker

PRESSED AND UNCOOKED
- Aged Gouda
- Cheddar
- Manchego

BLUE
- Stilton
- Roquefort

I found a few common flavors in the best pairings on page 103: buttered toast, bacon burger, ice cream. Because cheese is already a dairy product, it's unusual to pair milk chocolate with it. But in my taste tests I discovered that the combination turned into something like a candy bar (think Milky Way or Twix), which was almost irresistible. Here are a few other funny, insightful comments from the tasting panel:

- "Deliciously Junior Minty"
- "Tropical fruit and mangoes"
- "Buttered toast with jam and honey"
- "Pot roast and mashed potatoes"
- "Nutty and malty"
- "Fennel frond in tea"
- "Eating a stick of butter, in a good way"
- "Banana split with peanuts and hot fudge"

Chocolate and Bread

Joanna Brennan, cofounder of Pump Street Bakery, a bean-to-bar maker and bakery in the UK, told me a story a while back about how her mother used to ride her bicycle to a park and eat a baguette stuffed with chocolate. It had inspired her for years, and, I have to say, it inspired me to immediately do the same thing. The result was even more delicious than I could have imagined.

Though we've all been slathering Nutella on everything for years, not many people in the United States have tried to pair solid chocolate bars with bread. But they should! As Joanna says, the salt in bread brings out malty caramelization, two flavors that you'll also find in chocolate. In my experiments I encountered a few common flavors: cake, peanut butter and jelly, and marshmallows. Here are other insightful comments from the tasting panel:

- "A filled Danish"
- "Roasty and jammy"
- "Strawberry shortcake"
- "Beef jerky"
- "Caramelized peanuts"

CHOCOLATE & BREAD
PAIRINGS

DARK SALTED & MULTIGRAIN

TYPE OF CHOCOLATE	COMPLEMENTARY BREAD
Very Fruity and Bright *(such as Madagascar)*	• Baguette • Brioche
Smoky *(such as Papua New Guinea)*	• Brown sourdough • Rye, especially with caraway seeds
Nutty *(such as Venezuela, Central America, and Grenada)*	• Brioche
Floral *(such as Ecuador)*	• White sourdough
Dark Milk with salt	• Multigrain
Milk	• Brioche • Rye, especially with caraway seeds • Pumpernickel
Dried Fruit Inclusions	• White sourdough

When pairing these two together, be sure your bite of bread includes both the crust and crumb. You'll be tempted to chew immediately, and you might lose a bit of the nuance of the chocolate when you chew, but you'll gain something else great from the overall experience. I say go for it.

Fresh, warm bread is ideal for this pairing. If it's not warm, don't worry about heating it up, since the combo is just as good and I'd rather you not (as I did) toast or zap the bread beyond recognition.

ONE RULE: **The chocolate needs to be sweeter than the bread.** That's why it can be tricky to pair sweet breads like brioche with dark chocolate. Here are a few types of bread that go great with chocolate:

- Baguette
- Brioche
- Brown sourdough
- White sourdough
- Rye, especially with caraway seeds
- Multigrain
- Pumpernickel

COMPOSED CHOCOLATE PLATE

CHEESE GETS TO have all the fun. It's the ultimate party trick: pull out a cheese plate with fun accompaniments and everyone oohs and aahs. I've long wondered why chocolate should be any different. Sure, restaurants sometimes serve a "trio of chocolate desserts," but it's almost always something boring (yet delicious) like chocolate mousse and flourless chocolate cake. I say let the bars shine as they are, with a few accoutrements to bring out interesting flavor notes.

I've designed a specific composed chocolate plate opposite, but I hope you'll play around with your own combinations and create something truly unique. A few guidelines:

- Stick to four or five chocolates. Otherwise you'll overwhelm your guests and your palate.
- Pick different styles of chocolates to keep it interesting. A good rule of thumb is one dark, one milk, one white, one 100 percent, and one bonbon.

- A little bit goes a long way. Break up the bars before you serve them, and don't overwhelm the plate with too much of each chocolate.
- Serve the accompaniments on the side. You'll want to taste the chocolate separately and then with the goodies.

COMPOSED CHOCOLATE PLATE

100 percent dark chocolate
Dried figs

Single-origin Venezuela,
70 percent cocoa
Toasted walnuts
Fresh berries

Burnt
Caramel–
Amaro Truffles
(see recipe,
page 108)

Single-origin
Ecuador,
70 percent cocoa
Honey-Carrot
Purée
(see recipe,
page 112)

Baguette
Single-origin Madagascar,
70 percent cocoa
Manchego cheese (thinly sliced!)

Burnt Caramel–Amaro Truffles

Recipe from Recchiuti Confections

LEVEL:
Advanced

Yield

About
50 truffles

IT'S NO SURPRISE that boisterous chocolatier Michael Recchiuti's "signature flavor" is burnt caramel. I've been a huge fan of his for years, and when I met him recently with his wife, Jacky, we spent several hours talking about everything from his recent trip to Peru with Valrhona to Cheez Whiz–laden cheesesteaks from his native Philadelphia.

This truffle combines the larger-than-life, addictive taste of burnt caramel with amaro, a liqueur that complements dark chocolate particularly well. Michael recommends using single-origin Ecuador, Madagascar, Colombia, or Venezuela (especially Sur del Lago) chocolate here, which gives you a range of flavors to play with. The recipe for the burnt caramel base will make about 2 cups, which is much more than you need for these measly 50 truffles, but don't worry: you can keep this stuff in the fridge forever and use it when you're making ganache, mixing drinks, or even topping ice cream. Also, don't worry about the sugar getting too dark; it's supposed to be burnt.

BURNT CARAMEL BASE

- 3½ cups sugar
- 1 cup water

TRUFFLES

- 14 ounces chocolate (61 to 65 percent cocoa), coarsely chopped
- ¾ cup Fernet-Branca (amaro)
- ⅔ cup heavy whipping cream
- ¼ cup plus 1 tablespoon burnt caramel base
- 6 tablespoons unsalted butter, very soft
- 1 teaspooon ground star anise (optional)
- 1 cup unsweetened cocoa powder

SPECIAL EQUIPMENT

Sieve or splatter guard
Blender

1. Begin by making the burnt caramel base. If your kitchen has an exhaust fan, turn it on. Put the sugar in a heavy-bottomed pot (use an unlined copper pot if you have one). Set over medium heat and cook, stirring occasionally with a wooden spoon, until the sugar melts.

2. Continue to cook, without stirring, until the sugar turns black, about 10 minutes. If any crystals form on the sides of the pan as the sugar darkens, wash them down with a wet pastry brush. Just before the sugar turns black, the sugar syrup may foam up. If it does, reduce the heat to low and, wearing an oven mitt, carefully stir it down. When the sugar syrup is ready, it will smoke and large bubbles will break on the surface.

3. While the sugar is cooking, bring the water to a boil in a small saucepan. When the sugar is black, remove it from the heat and put a sieve or splatter guard over it. Wearing an oven mitt, slowly pour the hot water into the sugar syrup a little at a time, stirring it together if necessary. The mixture will sputter and foam. Be careful, as it is very hot.

4. Let the syrup cool to room temperature. Transfer to a storage container, cap tightly, and refrigerate until needed.

5. When ready to make the truffles, lightly wet the bottom and sides of an 8-inch square baking pan with a pastry brush or paper towel. Then line the bottom and sides of the pan with plastic wrap.

recipe continues on next page

Burnt Caramel–Amaro Truffles

continued

6. Put the chocolate in a double boiler and heat, stirring occasionally, until it reaches 115°F (46°C). Remove from the heat.

7. While the chocolate is melting, stir the Fernet-Branca, cream, and burnt caramel base together in a small saucepan and heat to 115°F (46°C).

8. Combine the chocolate and cream mixtures in a blender and blend for about a minute. The truffle base (ganache) will thicken, becoming slightly less shiny, and will develop a puddinglike consistency. Add the butter and blend again.

9. Pour the ganache into the lined pan. Spread it as evenly as possible and then tap the pan on the counter to remove any air bubbles. Allow the ganache to cool at room temperature until it has set, 2 to 4 hours. Cover the pan with plastic wrap and refrigerate for at least 4 hours.

10. Lift the square of ganache from the pan, turn it over onto a clean work surface, and remove the plastic wrap. Turn the ganache square over again and trim the edges. Cut the ganache into 1-inch squares using a knife you dip into hot water before each cut; wipe the knife dry before each cut and wipe it clean after each cut. Separate the pieces, put them on a pan lined with parchment paper, and cover them with plastic wrap. Refrigerate the squares for 24 hours before rolling them into truffles.

11. If you're using ground star anise, sift it together with the cocoa powder. Dust your palms with the cocoa powder, then roll the ganache squares into balls and coat them with the cocoa powder. Place the truffles in a container or plastic bag, adding enough of the cocoa powder to keep them from sticking. Store at room temperature, where they'll keep for up to 2 weeks, or in the freezer, where they'll keep for up to 6 months (see Chef's Tips, page 60, for detailed instructions).

Chocolatier Michael Recchiuti stands in his San Francisco store.

THOUGH MOST AMERICAN bean-to-bar makers have gotten their start in the past few decades, one dates back to the mid-1800s, when Etienne Guittard came to California from France in the hopes of striking it rich in the gold rush. He brought with him some chocolate from his uncle's factory and discovered that chocolate was in almost as high a demand as gold. He soon opened his own factory in 1868, on Sansome Street in San Francisco, and the company has been a California fixture ever since. It's also remained a family company: Gary Guittard, Etienne's great-grandson, is the current president, and he runs the company along with his daughter Amy and nephew Clark.

In addition to making delicious bars for every chocolate lover, Guittard has long focused on chocolate for professional chefs and chocolatiers; look closely and you'll see that well-known brands like See's Candies use their chocolate. That's because Guittard concentrates on flavor. Gary in particular is a champion of fine-flavor cocoa and bean-to-bar makers, and under Gary's leadership, Guittard was the first American company to make single-origin chocolate. He also spearheaded a grassroots campaign in 2007 called "Don't Mess with Our Chocolate" that effectively blocked an attempt by the FDA and big chocolate manufacturers to allow cheaper fats to replace cocoa butter and still call the resulting product chocolate. Today Gary continues to donate time and energy to making sure that chocolate will taste great for generations to come.

Honey-Carrot Purée

Recipe from Recchiuti Confections

LEVEL:
Easy

Yield

About
1½ cups

VEGETABLES AND CHOCOLATE are a divisive subject: either you're willing to experiment, or you're not. Keep in mind that Michael developed this recipe specifically to accompany solid chocolate bars for my composed chocolate plate. He says that any floral, light honey will work in it, but avoid pungent honey like buckwheat. A dash of salt and pepper helps bring out the depth of the carrots. Michael recommends fleur de sel, a particular type of sea salt, but you can use any fine-grained sea salt. I like this with a super-floral single-origin Ecuador chocolate, and Michael recommends single-origin Dominican Republic — either way, about 70 percent cocoa.

Try the chocolate and purée separately, then together, putting the chocolate in your mouth first, according to the milk-shake method described on page 92. You could also try making this purée with red or yellow beets in place of the carrots, as their sweetness will also pair well with chocolate.

1 **pound carrots, diced**
2 **tablespoons honey**
   Fleur de sel and freshly ground black pepper

SPECIAL EQUIPMENT
Food processor or blender

1. Bring a pot of water to a boil, then reduce the heat to a simmer. Add the carrots and cook until they are very soft, 10 to 15 minutes. Drain the carrots, transfer them to an ice-water bath, and let chill for 3 minutes to stop the cooking process.

2. When they are cooled, drain the carrots and transfer to a food processor or blender. Process until smooth. Add the honey and process until the mixture achieves a light whipped texture. Season with salt and pepper to taste.

How to
THROW A CHOCOLATE TASTING PARTY

NOW THAT YOU'RE a pro at tasting and pairing chocolate, it's time to throw a chocolate tasting party! Grab a few of your closest (and luckiest) friends and a couple of chocolate bars, and plan a fun evening with these tips.

1. **KEEP IT EXCLUSIVE**. Keep the number of people and the number of chocolates to a minimum to make sure things stay manageable. As with a composed chocolate plate (see page 106), you'll want to choose just four or five chocolates.

2. **CHOOSE YOUR CHOCOLATE**. I like to select bars that complement or contrast one another so that people can really taste the differences. Sometimes I'll pick five different single-origin bars to focus on the terroir of different places; other times I'll pick five bars of the same origin made by different companies to emphasize the chocolate-making process. Or, if there's one maker whose chocolate I love, I'll choose five of its bars to explore that maker's style. It's totally up to you, and there's no right or wrong way to do it. Go wild!

3. **PREP AHEAD OF TIME**. Make sure the chocolate is at room temperature before the party starts, and plan to serve each person about 5 grams of each bar. (For reference, the average bar is about 55 grams, so one bar will go a long way!) Cut up or break the bars and place each type of chocolate on its own plate. Or, if you're super fancy, create a special plate for each guest. Be sure to serve lemon water, sliced green apples, and/or soda crackers as palate cleansers.

4. **GO FORTH AND TASTE**. Try the chocolates one at a time, using the tasting guidelines on page 80. As a rule of thumb, you'll want to taste dark chocolates first, then milk, then white. As everyone tries each chocolate, talk about what you discover. Offer pens and paper so that people can take notes. Last but not least, throw in a few interesting pairings from this chapter to mix things up and keep it lively. This is chocolate, after all. Have fun with it!

CHAPTER FOUR

CHOCOLATE SNOBS
DON'T ✍ EAT
MILK
CHOCOLATE

(and other myths, debunked)

I HAVE A CONFESSION: I love milk chocolate. It was my first love, and it's often my treat of choice — but as a writer specializing in chocolate, it's a fact I only whisper to close friends after making sure the room isn't bugged.

That's because for years milk chocolate has gotten the shaft. In fact, for years you weren't considered a serious chocoholic if you ate anything with milk in it. I can't tell you how many times I've heard snobby chocolate lovers tell me:

"I only eat dark chocolate."

"It's 85 percent dark for me!"

"I'm a 100 percent type of gal."

"Anything below 70 percent is simply not chocolate."

"Milk chocolate? Please. That stuff barely has 30 percent cocoa."

This type of misguided snobbery has gone on too long. It's time to set the record straight about milk chocolate, cocoa percentage, and more.

SHADES OF BROWN

MILK CHOCOLATE
Chocolate liquor combined with sugar, milk powder, and/or cream powder. In the United States it must contain at least 15 percent cocoa.

DARK MILK CHOCOLATE
Milk chocolate with a higher-than-normal percentage of cocoa, usually around 60 percent. This allows for the depth of flavor of a semisweet chocolate with the creaminess and dairy element of a milk chocolate bar.

DARK CHOCOLATE
No legal definition in the United States. A form of semisweet or bittersweet chocolate, under the umbrella of *sweet chocolate*. Can contain milk products (!!!).

Myth
HIGH COCOA PERCENTAGE INDICATES QUALITY

MANY PEOPLE VIEW cocoa percentage as a mark of quality, as in, the higher the percentage, the higher quality the chocolate. This is just NOT TRUE.

Cocoa percentage simply measures the amount of the bar that comes from cocoa beans, whether that's **cocoa solids** or cocoa butter. So a 70 percent chocolate means that 70 percent of the bar came from cocoa beans and 30 percent came from added ingredients like sugar, vanilla, soy lecithin, or inclusions. *It is not related to quality in any way.*

So why doesn't every 70 percent bar taste the same? Well, makers have unique (often secret) recipes for their bars. One 70 percent bar could include 50 percent cocoa solids and 20 percent cocoa butter; another could include 30 percent cocoa solids and 40 percent cocoa butter (that would create a very smooth, buttery bar!). To make it even more complicated, different types of beans naturally contain different amounts of cocoa butter. Some are more lean, others more fatty. A bean's natural "butteriness" will change the consistency of the resulting chocolate.

Myth
MILK CHOCOLATE IS
LESSER CHOCOLATE

AS I SAID earlier, milk chocolate can be delicious. So why does it have such a bad reputation? As Fruition Chocolate's Bryan Graham put it, "Most milk chocolates are sickly sweet, with very little actual chocolate in them." Culinary historian and chocolate educator Alexandra Leaf agreed: "Most milk chocolate that the average person would be exposed to is low-quality, commercial, bad milk chocolate."

But if it's made well, milk chocolate can taste great. If you start with quality cocoa beans, treat them with care, and add quality sugar and milk powder, you can create a fantastic bar — one with as much or more depth of flavor than any dark chocolate. "Milk chocolate," expert Clay Gordon writes in *Discover Chocolate*, "is the white Zinfandel of the chocolate world: it doesn't get the respect it deserves."

But now all of that is changing, because milk chocolate is cool again. American bean-to-bar makers have started creating "dark milk chocolate" bars, and they are seriously delicious.

But wait, let's back up a minute. Did I just blow your mind? How can a chocolate be both dark and milk?

Good question. *Dark chocolate* doesn't technically mean anything. It doesn't have a formal definition, according to the USDA. Instead it actually falls under the umbrella term *sweet chocolate*, which can include up to 12 percent milk solids. Yes, dairy in dark chocolate!

These new "dark milk" bars generally contain a higher percentage of cocoa than traditional milk bars — usually around 60 percent, compared with 30 percent. They generally taste milder and creamier than a pure dark chocolate bar, but they retain all the complexity.

THE BEST DARK MILK CHOCOLATE

WANT TO EXPLORE the dark milk side? Try a bar from one of these artisan makers.

FRUITION

All about the Flavor

BRYAN GRAHAM makes milk chocolate. And white chocolate. He uses vanilla. He even makes truffles and dark-chocolate-coated, jalapeño-dusted corn nuts. CORN NUTS. In other words, Bryan Graham isn't like most craft chocolate makers, who tend to focus on two-ingredient, single-origin dark bars.

Of course, Bryan makes a pretty badass dark chocolate too. But it's his Marañón Canyon Dark Milk bar, a combination of milk and dark, that's winning gobs of awards, including a Gold medal at the 2016 World Finals of the International Chocolate Awards. This is the story of that bar.

I remember the first time I tried it. Jessica Ferraro of Bar Cacao had invited me to her house in San Francisco for a chocolate tasting. "I have a chocolate closet," she said

conspiratorially. I was sold. As we lay lazily on her couch surrounded by dozens of open bars, I thought it couldn't get any better. Then she opened a brand-new package and handed me a square without any comment. The mild chocolate started melting on my tongue almost immediately, the fruity notes tempered by traces of walnut, all laced with a hint of milk. It was magnificent. It was also my first dark milk chocolate.

Fruition Chocolate makes several milk chocolates, light and dark. "It's a great gateway for people to get into more flavorful, unique dark chocolates," Bryan said. In fact, he only made a Marañón milk bar because his Marañón single-origin dark chocolate wasn't selling that well. "I had extra beans and wanted to do something else with them," he told me. "I didn't know of anyone making a milk chocolate bar using those beans."

Those delicious beans. Craft chocolate makers always use special beans, but in this case they're extra special: they're a type called Nacional, a prized variety known for its fruity flavors that until recently were thought to be specific to Ecuador. But when a man named Dan Pearson was tromping through the jungle in Peru looking for bananas to import to the United States, he discovered a place called Marañón Canyon bursting with untouched cacao and a crazy-high percentage of white beans. "Our guide said, 'Around here, they're all like that,'" Dan remembered. "We went back to civilization and Googled it." Eventually he started buying wet beans from the area's farmers and fermenting and drying the beans himself. His company, Marañón, sells the beans to

Bryan taste-testing drying beans in Belize (left); the counter at Fruition's satellite shop in Woodstock, NY (right)

makers all over the world and makes its own chocolate as well.

Now those rare beans are in high demand, with chocolate makers scrambling to get their hands on them. Eric Ripert, chef and co-owner of Le Bernardin in New York City, calls it "the best chocolate in the world," and in 2012, with Anthony Bourdain, he made his own bar with it (before you go searching, it's not available anymore).

"It was the most expensive cocoa that we'd ever purchased," Bryan told me. "But I thought I could do something fun with it."

The result? A fun yet serious dark milk chocolate that blows away both casual and serious chocolate eaters.

These days, Bryan is still after fun. Case in point: recently he tried making a milk chocolate with dried candy cap mushrooms. "They taste and smell exactly like maple syrup," he said mischievously. "My idea is to mold a bar with caramelized pecans so it's maple-pecan flavor without any maple syrup in it. We'll see how it turns out. It might be disgusting."

I doubt it. Bryan understands both how to work with cocoa beans and how to mold the resulting chocolate into myriad delicious forms. "Why not play around with it?" he said when I asked him about using vanilla, making white chocolate and bonbons, and experimenting with things like mushrooms. "I don't like the idea of limiting myself and limiting what we can do."

Olive Oil–Sourdough Truffles

Recipe from Fruition Chocolate

LEVEL:
Advanced

Yield

30
truffles

AFTER MOVING TO New York City, I learned quickly that one of the best places to escape was upstate New York. One of the main reasons? Fruition Chocolate. Visit the bean-to-bar maker's store in Shokan and you'll find all sorts of deliciousness, including a rotating selection of truffles. Recently I was wowed by these truffles, which incorporate two unusual ingredients — olive oil and sourdough — into a delicious treat: the olive oil makes the ganache super creamy, and the entire truffle is rolled in sourdough breadcrumbs.

Fruition's Bryan Graham uses his Hispaniola bar, made with cocoa from the Dominican Republic, in this recipe, but it works well with any fruity chocolate. Also be sure to use high-quality extra-virgin olive oil (think Spanish); since it's one of only a few ingredients, it makes a big difference here. You can use store-bought breadcrumbs instead of making your own, but be sure to get fresh and preferably locally made ones instead of the packaged-and-preserved variety.

If you're sick of tempering chocolate but want to make truffles, this recipe might be for you. You'll still have to temper chocolate to make the ganache, but below the standard recipe, I've provided an alternative way to coat the truffles in chocolate without tempering yet more of the sweet stuff.

FOR THE GANACHE

- 8¾ ounces dark chocolate (70 percent cocoa), chopped
- ¾ cup plus 5 teaspoons extra-virgin olive oil

TO COAT THE TRUFFLES

- About 6 slices sourdough bread
- 1 pound dark chocolate (70 percent cocoa)

SPECIAL EQUIPMENT

Pastry bag (for a DIY version, see Chef's Tips, page 60)

recipe continues on next page

Olive Oil–Sourdough Truffles
continued

1. For the ganache, temper the chocolate, following the instructions on page 11.

2. Stir the oil into the tempered chocolate and blend well (preferably with an immersion blender, but by hand will work too). The ganache will be very liquidy. Place in the refrigerator and let chill for 2 to 4 hours, until it's firm but not solid.

3. Line a baking sheet with parchment paper. Transfer the ganache to a pastry bag and pipe into quarter-size balls on the baking sheet. As you pipe, keep the bag about ¼ inch above the paper so it doesn't touch or stick to the paper. Cover the balls with plastic wrap and place in refrigerator until firm, 1 to 2 hours.

4. Using your hands, roll each rough ball into a more-rounded ball. Some people like to wear gloves here, because this step is kind of sticky and messy. (Sorry, not sorry.) Place in the freezer overnight to harden.

STEP 3

5. The next day, when you're ready to finish the truffles, preheat the oven to 325°F (163°C). Cut the sourdough into 1-inch chunks and place on a baking sheet. Toast in the oven until dry, about 20 to 30 minutes. Let cool.

6. Cover a baking sheet with parchment paper. Pulse the toasted bread in a food processor until you have small crumbs, then pour the crumbs onto the lined baking sheet, spreading them out evenly.

7. Temper the chocolate for the coating, following the instructions on page 11. Line a second baking sheet with parchment paper.

8. Take the truffles out of the freezer and drop them, one at a time, into the warm tempered chocolate. Using a fork to guide it, roll the ball over once so that it's completely coated in the melted chocolate. Balance it on the fork, bouncing or shaking it lightly to remove any extra chocolate, then wipe the bottom of the fork against the edge of the bowl to remove any remaining extra chocolate.

9. Roll the ball in the bread crumbs to coat. Transfer to the lined baking sheet.

10. Let the truffles sit at room temperature until the chocolate coating is set, which should take 5 minutes or less. Enjoy!

COATING TRUFFLES WITH UNTEMPERED CHOCOLATE

To coat the ganache in untempered chocolate: Before removing the balls from the freezer (step 8), melt the 1 pound of dark chocolate in a microwave or double boiler and add 1 tablespoon olive oil. Mix well. Coat the truffles as described. If you go this route, store the truffles in the freezer (see the Chef's Tips, page 60), as the untempered chocolate will bloom quickly if it's stored at room temperature.

CHOCOLATE ISN'T CHOCOLATE

S OME PEOPLE WILL tell you that white chocolate is not actually chocolate because it doesn't contain cocoa solids (i.e., the brown stuff). White chocolate primarily consists of sugar, milk or cream powder, and cocoa butter that has been separated from those cocoa solids. Yet in the United States, it is legally considered chocolate: in the early 2000s the Hershey Corporation and the Chocolate Manufacturers Association of the United States of America lobbied the FDA successfully. Since 2004 "white chocolate" has been considered chocolate, as long as it contains at least 20 percent cocoa butter, a minimum of 14 percent total milk solids and 3.5 percent milk fat, and a maximum of 55 percent sugar or other sweeteners. The European Union follows the same standards, except that there isn't a maximum on sugars and sweeteners.

White Chocolate–Hazelnut Mousse in Pineapple Cups

Recipe from Kristofer Kalas, pastry chef and chocolatier

LEVEL: *Advanced*

Serves

12

EVERY CHOCOLATE BOOK has a recipe for hazelnut-chocolate spread (homemade Nutella, if you will, called *gianduja* by professionals). I know why: it's a delicious combination! But at this point, it's also kind of tired. That's why I'm including this recipe from chocolatier and pastry chef Kristofer Kalas, which turns your expectations upside down by pairing hazelnut paste with white chocolate and pineapple. The bright tropical fruit creates a gorgeous bowl for the mousse, cutting its richness so you feel light and happy when you're finished (and, if you're like me, ready for a second cup).

I love that this recipe calls for real vanilla bean. Buy dried beans at your regular grocery store and slice one open lengthwise with a sharp knife, then use the point of the knife to scrape the tiny seeds off the bean. If you have trouble finding hazelnut paste, you can substitute hazelnut butter (they're really the same thing) or make your own by toasting hazelnuts and blending them in a food processor. And if pineapple isn't your jam, you can serve the mousse in elegant glasses or cups, each filled with about 4 to 5 ounces of the mousse. It's perfectly delightful plain, but Kristofer recommends dressing it up with cookie crumbles or other fresh fruit.

- 1 ripe (but not overripe) pineapple
- 3¾ cups heavy cream
- 1¾ cups chopped white chocolate
- 2½ teaspoons glucose syrup
- ½ cup hazelnut paste or butter
- 9 grams gelatin sheets (about 4 sheets)
  Seeds from ½ vanilla bean, or 1 teaspoon vanilla extract
- ¾ cup water
- 3⅓ tablespoons butter
- 2½ tablespoons sugar

SPECIAL EQUIPMENT
Pastry bag (for a DIY version, see Chef's Tips, page 60), hand mixer or stand mixer

recipe continues on next page

125

White Chocolate–Hazelnut Mousse in Pineapple Cups

continued

1. Using a serrated knife, trim and quarter the pineapple, removing and discarding the innermost core. Slice into thin pieces about an inch square. Place one slice in the bottom of a muffin cup and arrange a few more around the sides, overlapping. You want to create solid cups for the mousse that you'll put in them later. Repeat to fill the muffin pan. Cover with plastic wrap and freeze for a few hours.

2. With a hand mixer or in a stand mixer, whip the heavy cream to soft peaks. Transfer to a bowl and set in the refrigerator to keep cold.

3. Combine the white chocolate and glucose syrup in a double boiler and heat, stirring occasionally, until the chocolate is melted. (Or melt in the microwave, in short intervals.) Add the hazelnut paste and stir until smooth. Set aside.

4. Fill a large bowl with water and ice. One by one, add the gelatin sheets and submerge until they've softened, about 5 to 10 minutes.

5. Scrape the vanilla bean seeds into a saucepan. Add the water, butter, and sugar, and heat just to a boil. Remove the gelatin sheets from the ice water and add to the saucepan. Stir until dissolved. Transfer the mixture to a large bowl.

6. Pour the melted chocolate mixture into the large bowl. Cool to between 86 and 95°F (30 to 35°C). Then gently fold in the whipped cream. Transfer the mousse to a pastry bag.

7. Take the pineapple cups out of the freezer. Working quickly, fill the pineapple cups with the mousse. If the mousse cools too much, the gelatin will begin to set and the mousse will look broken (think oily).

8. Freeze thoroughly for 8 to 10 hours.

9. To unmold, warm the muffin pan by setting it in a tray of hot water, being careful not to splash the mousse. Remove the cups, transfer to a dry tray, cover in plastic wrap, and put them back in the freezer. Move them to the refrigerator 30 minutes to 1 hour before serving, so that the mousse begins to soften. If you prefer a harder mousse, you can also serve them frozen. They should keep for 2 weeks in the freezer.

Myth
VEGAN CHOCOLATE IS UNUSUAL

ATELY I'VE SEEN a lot of lists proclaiming that they've found the best vegan dark chocolate in the world. But here's something that shouldn't be a secret: if a plain dark chocolate bar (read: one without inclusions or milk) is made with high-quality ingredients, it should *by default* be vegan. As soon as you start to see dairy like butter oil or milk substitutes on the ingredients list, you know you're in trouble (see page 139 for more detail about words to avoid).

Now, there are a few craft chocolate companies that exclusively make vegan chocolate products, and those are kind of a different category. Charm School, Madre, and Raaka are good examples. They make some pretty cool coconut milk chocolate and don't use any animal products in their factories; for die-hard vegans, those distinctions can be important.

Of course, vegan doesn't necessarily mean healthy. But that's a different issue, and one that I won't get on my high horse about here.

Myth
SOY LECITHIN IS BAD FOR YOU

OY LECITHIN, an emulsifier derived from soybeans, is often found in chocolate. It makes chocolate extra smooth and helps cocoa butter stay stable so that the chocolate doesn't bloom. Some people don't like it because it's "artificial"; others are concerned because it is derived from soy, which is a major allergen and in some circles is thought to affect our health adversely (especially genetically modified soy). However, researchers have recently discovered that there is not enough soy protein residue in soy lecithin to create an allergic reaction, and if it's used in

chocolate, it comprises no more than 0.5 percent of the total weight (and often much less).

Regardless, most bean-to-bar makers avoid soy lecithin, and you'll be hard-pressed to find it on an ingredients label in craft chocolate. Some makers have moved to sunflower lecithin, while others choose to keep their bars above 70 percent cocoa (where there's enough natural cocoa butter that they don't have to use an emulsifier). At the end of the day, though, I see this as a personal decision, not an ethical one.

Myth
CHOCOLATE IS A MAGICAL CURE-ALL

HAVE A FANTASY in which I eat chocolate all day and am healthier and happier than I ever thought possible. Judging by the hundreds of articles published about chocolate's health benefits every year, this seems like a reality. It's true that cocoa has more antioxidants (in the form of polyphenols and flavanols) than red wine, tea, and many berries. Cocoa has the potential to, among other things, lower blood pressure, increase muscle function, improve metabolic function, improve cognition, and help guard against memory loss, and its anti-inflammatory effects are off the charts. That's exciting stuff!

But a lot of the studies cited to support these claims are — how do I put this — bunk. For example, in 2016 the *New York Times* reported that chocolate can boost physical performance based on a study of eight people. That tiny sample size isn't unusual in this kind of research. Further, many of the studies rely on questionnaires and other imperfect ways of gathering data, like asking participants how much chocolate they eat per week and whether it's milk or dark. I don't know about you, but I couldn't tell you how much chocolate I ate this past week with any accuracy, and even if I could remember, I might downplay it out of sheer embarrassment.

That's why, at Harvard Medical School, Dr. JoAnn Manson is conducting the first large-scale study on the ability of cocoa flavanols to reduce the risk of heart attacks, memory loss, strokes, and other illnesses. She's giving cocoa flavanols or a placebo to 18,000 people for four years, probably until about 2020, and monitoring the effects. People tend to think that the more antioxidants, the better. But that's simply not true. "More is not necessarily better, and in fact more can be worse," Manson explained. Based on prior research, she and her team have discovered that 600 milligrams of cocoa flavanols is the ideal amount to get the benefits and avoid side effects. But before you get jealous of these folks in the study, keep in mind that they're not gorging on chocolate; they're taking two pills of isolated flavanols per day. "Chocolate is not a reliable source of high amounts of cocoa flavanols," Manson said. In fact, it's harder than you'd think to get 600 milligrams of flavanols from actually eating the stuff. Here's why:

- Depending on the type of cacao, there can be a **50 percent** variation in polyphenols.
- The fermentation process reduces the polyphenols by **up to 50 percent**.

- Sun-drying the beans reduces the remaining polyphenols by **up to 25 percent**.
- Roasting the beans reduces the remaining polyphenols by **up to 20 percent**.
- Grinding and refining the nibs into chocolate liquor reduces the polyphenols by **up to 10 percent**.

Okay, but let's say you still want to eat chocolate to get some good stuff in your diet. To get 600 milligrams, the ideal amount of flavanols, each day you'd need to eat . . .

CHOCOLATE FOR HEALTH

TO REACH 600 MILLIGRAMS YOU'LL NEED TO EAT:

COCOA POWDER
5 TABLESPOONS
56 Calories

DARK CHOCOLATE
3.8 OUNCES
600 Calories

OR

SEMISWEET CHIPS
4.4 OUNCES
½ CUP
592 Calories

OR

MILK CHOCOLATE
2 POUNDS,
OR 1.5 OUNCES
× 20½
1.5 OZ. 4,680 Calories

OR

Man, that's a lot of calories. As Manson said, "Having chocolate in moderation is perfectly fine as a treat, but I don't think it should be considered a health food."

Myth
RAW CHOCOLATE IS REAL

BET YOU'RE LOOKING at that info on the previous page about the way the chocolate-making process reduces polyphenols and thinking, *Okay, let's just eat a lot of raw cacao!* You wouldn't be alone. The **raw cacao** and raw chocolate movement is alive and well in this country, with so many gorgeous Instagram photos that I'm constantly craving chocolate. The only problem? Most of that stuff isn't raw. I could rant about it here, but instead I'd like to let Raaka, a great Brooklyn-based bean-to-bar company, tell the story . . .

RAAKA
Lust for Unroasted Chocolate

RASPBERRY LEMONADE doesn't make me think of chocolate. But when Raaka, the Brooklyn-based maker headed up by Nate Hodge and Ryan Cheney, released their raspberry-lemonade chocolate bar in 2016, they told me it was officially "the most Raaka bar" of all time. Why? Because instead of roasting out the acetic acid of Madagascar beans, they kept the lemony intensity and raised it one by adding freeze-dried raspberries. That creative way of using unroasted beans, of embracing their flavor, with youthful whimsy — well, that's Raaka.

Cofounder and chocolate maker Nate Hodge carefully picks a cacao pod off a tree in the Dominican Republic.

Because they don't roast their beans, the company calls their chocolate "virgin." But they don't call it "raw," which some might dismiss as hipster pretentiousness but others will understand addresses a deeper problem: "raw" chocolate is hardly ever really raw. Ryan and Nate had started out wanting to make raw chocolate, and they bought their ingredients from, among other places, Essential Living Foods, one of the biggest providers of raw cocoa powder and cocoa butter. But in 2009, Essential Living Foods discovered that its products were actually being processed at temperatures over 118°F (48°C), which is generally considered the upper limit for raw processing. They came clean and changed providers and procedures, but the scandal was a lesson for everyone: you don't always know what you're being sold.

It's still a huge problem in the raw chocolate world, and experts advise taking the word *raw* with a grain of salt. There aren't any legal standards for the word, and there isn't any third-party certification either. It's tricky if not near impossible to keep cocoa beans below 118°F (48°C) during the fermentation and drying process; meanwhile, roasting is out, and grinding and refining must be done very carefully. Ryan noted that he'd been to restaurants and shops selling chocolate labeled "raw" even years after the Essential Living Foods scandal. "It was b.s.," he said, "and it still is b.s."

In other words, Ryan and Nate (who answered a Craigslist employment ad shortly after Ryan started and has been essential ever since) felt tricked. But rather than give up, Ryan said they decided to pursue a quest of minimally processing their ingredients to "see what flavors we feel are amazing and also made without roasting cocoa beans."

continued on next page

R A A K A continued

"It's about harnessing the flavor of the raw beans," Nate said. "We want to transport people." Other makers roast the beans to remove unwanted acids and off-flavors, but Raaka has to temper and work with those tastes directly. Think vibrant berries and tropical fruits as well as mushroom and smoke, depending on the beans. Raaka pairs those strong flavors with interesting inclusions and natural sugars, resulting in bars with flavors like Bourbon Cask Aged (which won a Good Food Award), Maple and Nibs, Yacón (an alternative sugar), Coconut Milk, and Smoked Chai. Some in the chocolate world look down on inclusions, but the reality is that folks love them. In my opinion, inclusions, like blends, are an art form. Consider, for example, the pairing of earthy Bolivian beans with smoked tea to arrive at a unique flavor profile for that Smoked Chai bar, and the marriage of berry-tasting cocoa beans from the Oko-Caribe co-op in the Dominican Republic with

Chocolate maker Victoria Canonico scrapes chocolate off a roll mill (left); chocolate maker Hector Hernandez grinds sea salt onto finished chocolate bars (right).

coconut milk to get a creamy, bright flavor for Raaka's Coconut Milk bar.

Some people in the bean-to-bar world say that Raaka doesn't make real chocolate because roasting cocoa is an essential step. Director of marketing William Mullan likens that attitude to the idea that gay marriage isn't really marriage because it's not between a man and a woman. "In fact," he said, "people think we make pretty damn good chocolate." It's true: look almost anywhere these days, from Whole Foods Market to specialty stores to cute boutiques, and you'll find the progressive company's bars.

Of course, it's not all about the bottom line. "I'm not interested in business for business's sake," Ryan said. "My interest is in finding innovative ways to make a more positive social impact in the world, and I see business as a vehicle to do that."

Nate echoed that sentiment: "When you communicate with Raaka, that communication should be joyful and enriching and not just a transaction." That's why, for example, the company spends so much time working directly with farmers to source beans ethically. It's also why their factory is open for tours or the casual drop-in to taste and talk about chocolate.

All this philosophy can be condensed into one word: *raaka*. "It's Finnish," Ryan explained. "It can mean raw, like an uncooked vegetable. It can also mean raw like a blustery, cold wind in your face. Or like someone who has a personality that's strong. It's a broad definition for the word *raw*."

CHAPTER FIVE

LABELING
and the
ART *of* DESIGN

BUYING A BAR of chocolate shouldn't be an academic exercise, but with the maze of labels available these days, it's hard not to stand dumbfounded in the chocolate aisle. Most of us resort to the same tactic we use to buy wine: pick the prettiest package! Of course we shouldn't judge a book by its cover, but sometimes it's tempting. Especially when the packaging of so many artisan bars is so beautiful.

But before we get to that, let's talk about what to look for on a chocolate label, as well as what all that labeling terminology means. This cheat sheet will help you look like a bona fide chocolate expert.

The brand name may be accompanied by words like "small-batch," "craft," "artisan," or "handmade" to indicate that this isn't your run-of-the-mill, mass-produced chocolate.

Most craft chocolate notes where its cocoa comes from.

The label should identify the cocoa percentage.

Batch numbers are usually pretty small, and sometimes makers will even write the numbers by hand.

Expiration dates for chocolate work like those for other foods: the fresher, the better.

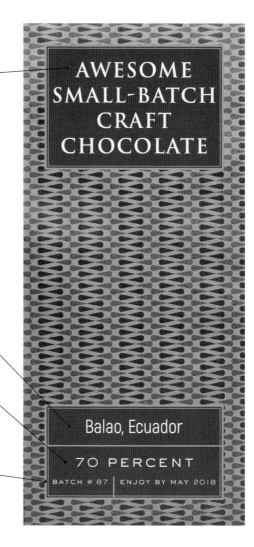

AWESOME
SMALL-BATCH
CRAFT
CHOCOLATE

Balao, Ecuador

70 PERCENT

BATCH # 87 | ENJOY BY MAY 2018

We roast, crack, sort, winnow, grind, conche, and temper small batches of beans, then mold and wrap each bar by hand.

A bean-to-bar operation will generally identify itself as such.

Sourced Directly

Phrases like "direct trade" or "fair trade" indicate the company's relationship to the farmer; see chapter 6 for more details.

The beans in this bar come from the Camino Verde farm in Balao, Ecuador. We visited owner Vicente Norero in April 2016 and saw firsthand the time and care he puts into fermenting and drying cacao, ensuring that each batch lives up to its full potential and tastes amazing.

Generally, the more information, the better. It's common to find info about the farm if the cocoa is from a single estate.

YOU MIGHT TASTE:
fudge brownie, caramel, roasted nuts.

Tasting notes indicate the flavors the maker tastes in the bar and are meant to be a loose guide.

INGREDIENTS
COCOA BEANS, CANE SUGAR, MILK POWDER, COCOA BUTTER, VANILLA, SOY LECITHIN.

Cocoa beans should *always* be listed first. All of these ingredients are okay.

Label Smarts

Some of the shorthand used on labels can expand into a lot of information — and contention. For example, phrases like "small batch," "craft," "handmade," and "artisan" don't have legal definitions. Here are some things to keep in mind:

- Unlike in other parts of life, with chocolate, people like to brag about their small size. Based on conversations with larger bean-to-bar makers, I define **small batch** as chocolate made in batches up to 550 pounds, using a variety of equipment, but it's hard to find a definitive rule. Meanwhile, according to the International Chocolate Awards, a **microbatch** means the capacity of the largest machine in production is 110 pounds or less.
- Chocolate makers love to say everything is **handmade**, which, strictly speaking, means the food or product is made by hand, without the use of machines. Since it's almost impossible to make **fine chocolate** completely without a machine (especially when grinding nibs!), the term is another messy one without an agreed-upon definition. Common stages done by hand are sorting beans, filling bar molds, and wrapping bars.
- The same problems apply to the word **_artisan_**. Traditionally that word means a person who has apprenticed with a master to learn a trade and become a master herself, or a description of the products she makes. However, in the United States it's currently an undefined and shape-shifting word, used by makers and companies however they see fit. It's often seen as interchangeable with "craft," "small batch," and, in chocolate, "bean to bar." Every maker uses it differently, but consumers associate it overwhelmingly with flavor and being handmade. Take "handmade" and "artisan" with a grain of salt, since they often promise more than they deliver.
- Cocoa percentage simply means the percentage of cocoa solids and cocoa butter in a chocolate. A higher percentage doesn't mean higher quality, but including this information means the maker is paying attention.
- Direct-trade sourcing is ideal, but you'll often see other qualifications and certifications on labels, such as fair trade and Rainforest Alliance. Investigate these standards carefully before assuming they guarantee ethical and high-quality chocolate. (See chapter 6 for more information.)
- Tasting notes are suggestions, not the end-all, be-all. Some people read the notes before they taste, as guides; others wait to see what they taste and then read.

INGREDIENTS: SUGAR; VEGETABLE OIL [PALM OIL; SHEA OIL; SUNFLOWER OIL; PALM KERNEL OIL; AND/OR SAFFLOWER OIL]; NONFAT MILK; CORN SYRUP SOLIDS; ENRICHED WHEAT FLOUR [FLOUR; NIACIN; FERROUS SULFATE; THIAMIN MONONITRATE; RIBOFLAVIN; FOLIC ACID]; LACTOSE (MILK); CONTAINS 2% OR LESS OF: COCOA PROCESSED WITH ALKALI; WHEY (MILK); HIGH FRUCTOSE CORN SYRUP; CHOCOLATE; LECITHIN (SOY); BAKING SODA; SALT; NATURAL FLAVOR AND ARTIFICIAL FLAVOR; TOCOPHEROLS, TO MAINTAIN FRESHNESS; PGPR, EMULSIFIER. ⓤ D ALLERGY INFORMATION: MANUFACTURED ON THE SAME EQUIPMENT THAT PROCESSES ALMONDS.

Phrases to Avoid

Then there are the words that should never, ever appear on a quality chocolate label. If you see one of these hazards, don't panic! Follow the same guidelines you would if you came across a grizzly in the wilderness: carefully place the bar on the ground and back away slowly toward safety (a.k.a. a more delicious chocolate bar).

CHOCOLATY. If used as a product name, it means the bar doesn't contain enough cocoa (10 percent in the United States) to legally be called chocolate. It may also contain fats other than cocoa butter, artificial sweeteners, or milk substitutes, any of which would also prevent it from being legally designated "chocolate."

MADE WITH CHOCOLATE. Same issue as with "chocolaty."

CHOCOLATE LIQUOR. If you see this on an ingredients list, it means the company did not make the chocolate from the bean. That's not necessarily a bad thing, but if you're looking for bean-to-bar chocolate, this phrase should be avoided.

VEGETABLE OIL. A clear indicator that the chocolate is subpar, to the point

that, legally, it has to be called "chocolaty," not "chocolate."

BUTTER OIL. Clarified butter, which is often used instead of cocoa butter in cheap, low-quality chocolates.

ARTIFICIAL SWEETENERS. Stevia, Xylitol, Aspartame, Sucralose, and so on will give the chocolate a strange taste and should be avoided.

MILK SUBSTITUTES. Also an indicator that the chocolate is subpar and made by cutting corners.

PGPR. An acronym for polyglycerol polyricinoleate, which is made from glycerol, among other things. It's often used as an emulsifier in low-quality chocolates.

VANILLIN. The synthetic version of vanilla. It should be avoided.

DISTRIBUTED BY. Indicates that the chocolate was made by a big conglomerate, not a small-batch maker.

PRODUCT OF. If you're buying from an American company but the label says "product of Belgium" or "product of Switzerland," for example, the chocolate is made by a big corporation and then sold to the company you're buying from.

Balsamic Strawberries in Mini Chocolate Cups

LEVEL:
Medium

Yield

24 cups
(mini cupcake size)

Recipe from Clay Gordon, chocolate expert and founder of TheChocolateLife.com

THIS RECIPE COMES from chocolate expert Clay Gordon, and I'm addicted to its surprising combination: balsamic vinegar, black pepper, and chocolate, which all play off the natural sweetness of strawberries. Clay says to keep in mind that you don't need high-end balsamic or cocoa powder to make this treat; they both bow down to the strawberries, the real star. For the cups, use a nice fruity chocolate from an origin like Madagascar to complement the strawberries, a nutty chocolate from somewhere like Venezuela to contrast them, or a balanced blend to let the strawberries shine.

If you want to be fancy, you can use truffle molds, but I think mini cupcake pans and baking cups work just as well (if not better). Don't despair if a few cups break while you're making them: there's chocolate to spare in this recipe for just that occasion. You can use one pastry brush to make them, but I recommend two, since a single brush can sometimes get goopy with too much chocolate. Last but not least, you can make the syrup and cups ahead of time, but be sure to assemble them shortly before serving, since they will only hold up for a few hours.

recipe continues on next page

12 ounces dark chocolate (at least 70 percent cocoa), coarsely chopped

¾ cup balsamic vinegar

½ cup sugar

¼ cup unsweetened natural cocoa powder

1 pound strawberries, cut into thin matchsticks

Freshly ground black pepper

SPECIAL EQUIPMENT: Two mini cupcake pans, foil mini baking cups

CHEF'S TIP

Save the leftover syrup to spoon over ice cream or other desserts.

CHOCOLATE CUPS

1. Melt the chocolate in a double boiler or microwave (in short intervals), stirring occasionally.

2. Set out 24 foil mini baking cups. Use a small pastry brush to paint a thin, even layer of melted chocolate inside the baking cups, leaving a roughly ⅛-inch border at the top. Place the chocolate cups in mini cupcake pans and freeze for 10 minutes.

3. Using a second brush, paint a second layer of chocolate inside the cups. If the melted chocolate has become too firm, place it over a pan of barely simmering water and stir until remelted. If you have any chocolate left over, paint a few extra cups, in case any break. Return the cups to the freezer for 10 minutes.

4. Store the cups in the refrigerator; they'll keep for 2 to 3 days.

SYRUP

1. Whisk together the vinegar, sugar, and cocoa powder in a small saucepan and bring to a boil.

2. Lower the heat and simmer, stirring occasionally, until the mixture is syruplike but not as thick as honey, 12 to 15 minutes. Watch the pan closely, lowering the heat as necessary if the mixture bubbles up. When it's done, remove from the heat and let cool.

ASSEMBLY

1. A few hours before you're ready to serve the cups, combine the strawberries with ¼ cup of the balsamic syrup in a bowl and gently toss to coat. The strawberries should be only lightly coated in syrup, but if they seem dry, add more syrup. (Any leftover syrup can be stored in an airtight container in the refrigerator and will keep for at least 1 week.)

2. Immediately before serving, peel the foil off the outside of the chocolate cups. Divide the strawberries among the chocolate cups and garnish with freshly ground black pepper.

3. Eat the chocolate cups in a single bite!

Chocolate Pioneers
MAST BROTHERS

BEARDS. AND BEAUTIFUL PACKAGING.
That's probably what you know about Rick and Michael Mast, a pair of Brooklyn hipsters who in 2007 launched one of the first American bean-to-bar companies. The media-savvy brothers quickly became the toast of the town and the country, with splashy magazine stories and featured chocolate in boutiques, specialty stores, and grocery stores around the country. Famed chefs like Thomas Keller started using Mast chocolate in many restaurants, and the company inspired dozens of people like Scott Moore Jr. of Tejas Chocolate and Adam Dick and Dustin Taylor of Dick Taylor Chocolate (page 145) to start making their own chocolate. In particular, fans are drawn to the Mast Brothers' design aesthetic, especially the beautiful packaging.

However, at the end of 2015 a story broke that when Mast Brothers was getting started, the brothers had remelted Valrhona chocolate and sold it as their own. The brothers vehemently denied the accusations — and still do — but nevertheless, people were outraged, and the story quickly went viral.

Yet shortly after the debacle the company opened a massive new factory in Brooklyn and launched a new line of bars that doesn't include much information about the origins of the cocoa beans (highly unusual in the bean-to-bar world, where transparency is valued). Meanwhile its Los Angeles and London locations shuttered in early 2017. The scandal called into question the authenticity of all artisan goods, not just chocolate, creating distrust that has lingered long past the news cycle. As Rick told me recently, "Hershey's and Cadbury are laughing all the way to the bank watching these craft chocolate makers destroy each other."

Iced Spicy Drinking Chocolate

From Chocolopolis

THIS RECIPE COMES from one of my favorite specialty shops in the country, Chocolopolis, in Seattle. Owner Lauren Adler's collection of craft chocolate makes it a must-stop when I visit the Emerald City, and the crazy-good café offerings are just whipped cream on the drinking chocolate. I especially like this recipe, which adds heat to a traditional beverage for a nice surprise. The Aztecs took their chocolate with added spices like chiles and allspice and very little sugar. Lauren adapted that idea for a modern palate, adding milk and sugar, but you still get the idea.

Be sure to use chile flakes (large pieces of dried chiles), not powdered chiles. Flakes offer a lot of great flavor, and you can strain them out easily so the chocolate is not gritty. If you can't find flakes, substitute half the amount of ground spices and strain the drink extra carefully. Be sure to use a smoky or earthy chocolate that can stand up to chiles, like single origins from Mexico, Papua New Guinea, or Venezuela.

8 ounces dark chocolate (preferably 72 percent cocoa or darker), chopped

4 cups whole milk

2½ teaspoons ancho chile flakes

2½ teaspoons guajillo chile flakes

1½ teaspoons whole allspice berries

Pinch of cayenne pepper

1. Combine the chocolate, milk, ancho and guajillo chile flakes, allspice, and cayenne in a saucepan and heat over medium heat. Stir continuously to prevent burning or boiling the milk.

2. When the chocolate is melted and steam begins to rise off the top, take the saucepan off the stove, cover, and set aside to steep for 20 minutes. If you're short on time, you can reduce the amount of steeping time, but the flavor will be less intense.

3. When the chocolate has finished steeping, place the saucepan back on the stovetop and heat over medium heat, stirring continuously, until steam begins to rise.

4. Remove the saucepan from the heat and strain the mixture through a fine-mesh strainer.

5. Cool for 10 minutes, then pour over ice and enjoy!

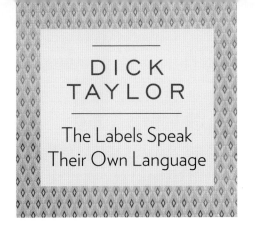

DICK TAYLOR

The Labels Speak Their Own Language

DUSTIN TAYLOR AND ADAM DICK make the kind of chocolate that you'll cross a room for. But their labels are what will inspire you to notice them in the first place. Their brand, Dick Taylor Craft Chocolate, captures the youthfulness of the new American chocolate movement while maintaining its spirit of simplicity and a homegrown attitude — all with images of boats and the sea.

The process hasn't been easy, though. In the beginning Adam and Dustin bought every bean-to-bar chocolate they could find and looked at the labels. "Ninety percent had a brown wrapper," Dustin said. "Ninety percent were glossy, and a large portion had some kind of cacao pod or Mayan imagery on it. Lots of them are some iteration of the word *chocolate* with X's and L's and O's and C's — stuff you can't even pronounce."

"Okay," they said. "So we're going to do everything exactly the opposite of that."

Starting with the idea of a pattern like "argyle socks" and texture like wood shavings, Dustin reached out to his brother Garrett, a graphic designer and sketch artist who worked at Pixar. Boats immediately came into the picture because it's a huge passion for them: Adam and Dustin have even restored a "rusty old sailboat" to working condition and sailed it around Humboldt Bay. Garrett decided to go with a streamlined photo illustration in one color ("like the 1890s, but simple," Garrett said), with two figures in the foreground to provide an anchoring narrative. And on the back? "I wanted that to have more of a utilitarian look so that it felt really approachable, like a box of crackers from the 1930s," Garrett explained, saying he wanted customers to be able to immediately understand what they were looking at without wading through a lot of text and confusing terms.

Of course, DIY millennials like Adam and Dustin weren't just going to take Garrett's designs to Kinko's. Through Craigslist, they found a foundering print shop in Oakland and drove all night to get there before anyone else could buy it. They loaded up 12,000 pounds of printing equipment at 2 a.m. and then hauled

continued on next page

Adam (left) and Dustin (right) at their factory in Eureka, California

DICK TAYLOR continued

it back to Eureka, California, their home base, where they taught themselves how to letter-press their own labels.

In other words, they're determined. Take the bar of chocolate itself. To create a seamless experience, Adam, Dick, and Garrett wanted to rework the actual shape and form of the chocolate. A standard bar of chocolate is usu-ally molded into lots of little squares, so you can easily break off a bite, piece by piece. "But chocolate breaks however it breaks," Garrett said. "So I started playing around with a dia-mond shape and just adding detail." Look at a Dick Taylor bar and you'll find diamonds on

diamonds, with curlicues in the middle of each and a bigger diamond in the center with the words "Dick Taylor Craft Chocolate" and a sim-plified image of a boat's sails.

To get the intricate mold to work, Adam and Dustin had to retemper the chocolate almost constantly, as well as play with its viscosity in order to get it to flow into every part of the mold correctly. "Early on we'd go day after day, tossing whole batches back, just trying to get it to work," Adam remembered. That threw a huge kink in the process, since if they couldn't temper and mold bars correctly, they couldn't very well sell them. A few years later, though, they've

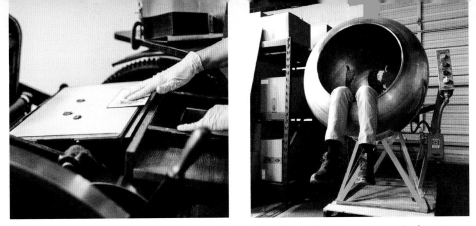

Dick Taylor letterpresses their own labels on a refurbished machine (left); Adam was so excited to get a new panning machine that he decided to hang out in it (right).

mostly figured it out, and Dustin says that now they only remold a few bars per batch. Still, that's quite a commitment for a small company and shows a dedication to quality and design.

Most impressively, the team has made this happen without spending a ton of money. At the 2015 Northwest Chocolate Festival in Seattle, makers talked about spending up to $1.50 per package. Dick Taylor, on the other hand, makes it happen for about 30 cents.

That's a huge difference for small businesses that sometimes barely make the bottom line.

Yet the end product feels expensive, hand-made, precious. "We want customers to feel like what they have in their hands is valuable," Garrett explained. "The shape of the package, the thickness of the paper, the feeling that it's worth the $8 or $9 that you spent on it. It's almost like when you buy [an Apple] product, like a new iPhone or iPad. There's something to the packaging — it's just a few simple elements that make it feel like whatever is inside is high quality."

CHOCOLATE AS ART: GORGEOUS BARS AND LABELS

Raaka

Fruition

Ritual

CHOCOLATE IS AS beautiful as it is delicious, and lately makers have ditched their old brown wrappers for creative patterns, bright colors, and marvelous molds. Mast Brothers was one of the first brands to do so, and its distinctive handmade paper labels have inspired many other makers to follow suit. Now the competition is getting stiff, with so many pretty packages that I sometimes feel I need to frame them after the chocolate is gone — or make some Willy Wonka–style wallpaper.

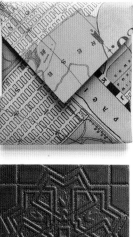

Map

FRENCH BROAD

Home Is Where the Chocolate Is

IN 2003 JAEL RATTIGAN was standing in her kitchen, making a recipe from Alice Medrich's cookbook *Bittersweet*, when she felt a strange tingling in her hands. "I looked at them and saw they were covered in chocolate," she remembered. "And I said aloud, 'Chocolate is the thing. Chocolate will make me happy.'"

Within a few months, she and her now husband Dan Rattigan dropped out of their respective grad programs in Minneapolis, bought an RV, converted it to run on used vegetable oil ("which we spent the summer collecting from the Dumpsters behind Chinese restaurants," Dan said), and drove to Costa Rica to start a new chocolate-filled life.

The pair opened a café called Bread and Chocolate, which quickly became a gathering place for the community. Eventually they made their way back to the States, and in 2008 they did it again: drive into downtown Asheville, North Carolina, and you'll find an impressive building with the words "French Broad Chocolate Lounge" displayed prominently.

And it's not just chocolate bars. Think chocolate cake. Chocolate brownies. Chocolate ice cream. Chocolate chip cookies. Chocolate mousse. Chocolate truffles. Drinking chocolates.

"In Costa Rica, we created an experience," Dan said. "We made a whole environment for people to enjoy our food, and that's how to make this [business] work. We wanted to create a sacred space for chocolate where we could invite people in and really immerse them in the experience."

Asheville loved the idea, and the café — named for the river that runs through the city — took off. At first it was enough to serve dessert, but soon Dan and Jael began to feel that something was missing. They were making everything from scratch — except the chocolate. "We were berries to jam, peanuts to peanut butter, flour to bread. We made everything from the most basic ingredients," Dan explained. "The idea of using someone else's chocolate — it never felt right to us." So after a few years of running the café, they started experimenting with making their own bean-to-bar chocolate. They've nailed it now, and there's so much demand for their bars that it's hard to find them outside Asheville.

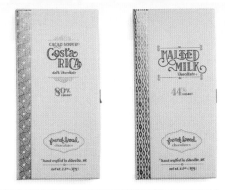

By November 2014 French Broad had officially outgrown its space, so Dan and Jael moved downtown into an even bigger building, expanded the café, and opened Chocolate + Milk, a coffee, ice cream, and chocolate bar shop next door that features a killer selection of American-made bean-to-bar chocolate.

The entire building is certified green, and they use environmentally friendly processes to ship their chocolates across the country. Dan and Jael are also committed to using local ingredients and trading directly with farmers in other countries. They partner with Bicycle Benefits to give customers a discount on their ice cream (or cake or cookies or bars) when they ride their bikes to the lounge. And they make a crazy assortment of mouthwatering desserts that, in my experience, are impossible to resist. In other words, they've designed a special space that embodies the ethos of progressive Asheville, as well as a diversified, people-pleasing product line that appeals to more than one type of customer. That's a radically different business model than most bean-to-bar chocolate makers subscribe to, where everything is about single-origin bars, and I believe that's why French Broad has been so successful.

In 2016 they added the final touch to their business: gorgeous packaging. Each label looks like a book, and opening it reveals, along with the chocolate, a small printed booklet with "chapters" that are unique to each kind of bar (for example, the sea salt bar includes a chapter on French Broad's local partner Bulls Bay Saltworks). Together they make a beautiful library of chocolate.

Truffle Torte

Recipe from French Broad Chocolate

CUSTOMERS HAVE LOVED this flourless chocolate torte from French Broad since the first day the bean-to-bar maker opened its Chocolate Lounge. It's something like a cross between a brownie, a cake, and a custard. Of course, that also means that a small slice of this super-rich torte goes a long way. Serve it warm or chilled (both ways are great), and top it with freshly whipped cream and berries.

French Broad uses a blend of Nicaraguan, Peruvian, and Guatemalan chocolate in their version of this recipe, but co-owner Jael Rattigan says she's made single-origin versions using those three types and all have turned out wonderful. In other words, it's a versatile recipe perfect for playing with different flavor profiles and/or showcasing your favorite chocolate.

15 **ounces chocolate (65 to 80 percent cocoa), chopped**

7 **ounces butter, chopped**

5 **eggs**

2 **tablespoons water**

½ **cup sugar**

1 **teaspoon salt**

**SPECIAL EQUIPMENT
9-inch springform pan,
hand mixer or stand mixer**

1. Preheat the oven to 350°F (177°C). Line the bottom of a 9-inch springform pan with parchment paper.

2. Melt the chocolate and butter in a double boiler or microwave (in short intervals), stirring occasionally. Pour the chocolate-butter mixture into the bowl of a stand mixer (or just a large bowl if you're using a hand mixer).

3. Add the eggs and mix at low speed, scraping the bowl as needed, until the mixture is completely smooth, 2 to 5 minutes.

4. Pour the water into a small saucepan, then add the sugar and salt. Cook over medium-low heat until the sugar and salt dissolve (a minute or two), swirling the pan to aid in even cooking.

5. With the mixer at low speed, stream the melted sugar mixture into the chocolate mixture. When all the sugar is incorporated, turn the mixer up to medium-high speed and mix until the batter is smooth and shiny, about 3 minutes.

6. Scrape the batter into the springform pan. Bake for 30 to 35 minutes, until the edges look set but the center still looks shiny. Let cool before serving.

CHAPTER SIX

ETHICS
FOR THE
NEXT
CENTURY

SO FAR WE'VE talked a lot about taste and how bean-to-bar makers concentrate on the many flavor notes in chocolate. But there's another idea that defines the bean-to-bar movement: connection and community.

It's not just about rebuilding a connection to food and the process of making it. It's also about rebuilding a connection among people. Community is vital to these new makers. And "community" means so much more than direct neighbors. It means taking responsibility for the whole world, for our global "brothers and sisters," as Shawn Askinosie, the founder of Askinosie Chocolate, says. That's why recently so many craft chocolate makers have changed the way they do business, rejecting fair trade, the status quo system, in favor of a new model called direct trade. Direct trade allows makers to cultivate face-to-face relationships with farmers and have a direct effect on the international landscape. It also allows them to guarantee better-tasting ingredients, bringing us full circle back to flavor.

WHY CHOCOLATE SHOULDN'T COST $1

W'RE USED TO PAYING about $1 for a bar of chocolate. But that price undercuts the farmer, the flavor, and the finesse that it takes to make good chocolate. To understand why many craft chocolate makers have adopted the direct-trade model — and higher prices — let's look at how Big Chocolate works with farmers.

Chocolate has a sordid past and present, full of human rights violations like slavery, indentured servitude, and abject poverty. As Europeans developed a taste for chocolate back in the day, and industrialization made it easy to produce chocolate by the ton, millions of Africans were enslaved to work cacao farms in Central and South America as well as the Caribbean and Africa. For example, on the West African island of São Tomé in the nineteenth century, more than 100,000 Africans labored on cacao plantations; though slavery was formally abolished in 1876, their descendants worked as de facto slaves until 1975, when the island gained independence from Portugal.

Today about 70 percent of the world's chocolate comes from Africa, mostly Ghana and Ivory Coast, where human rights abuses still run rampant. A BBC documentary in 2000 exposed egregious human rights abuses on Ivory Coast

cacao plantations. Recently the media has focused on the most blatant problem: child labor and slavery. "They are enjoying something that I suffered to make," a little boy who had been farming cacao since he was five years old told the camera when asked what he thought about people gobbling chocolate in the rest of the world. "They are eating my flesh."

Big brands like Nestlé, Mondelēz, and Hershey have introduced programs to help improve farmers' lives and reduce child labor, and they have banded together to form CocoaAction, a group dedicated to improving productivity, sustainability, and community development through training programs. And they're working to meet US lawmakers' requirements to reduce child labor in West Africa by 70 percent by 2020. Yet despite industry attempts at reform, the problem has only gotten worse, with a 21 percent increase in child labor in cacao production between 2009 and 2014.

But the issue is complicated. Focusing on child labor and slavery alone will not fix the underlying problems. Whether or not the many children working on cacao plantations are outright slaves, they may have no other choice but to work alongside the rest of their family on farms, all using machetes to harvest and crack pods — something that's risky even for adults — to survive. The hard truth is, many African cacao farmers are subsistence farmers living in extreme poverty. In Tanzania, for example, almost one-third of the population lives below the poverty line.

This kind of poverty is unacceptable no matter what, but it is especially alarming when we take into account the fact that demand for chocolate is growing and the price of beans is rising. Despite the increasing demand, farmers are being paid less: in the 1980s they received 16 percent of the retail price of chocolate, but now they receive only 3 to 6 percent. In 2016 a California district court dismissed lawsuits accusing Nestlé and Hershey of neglecting to disclose that the cocoa in some of their brands could have come from slave labor; the judge said it wasn't for the courts to decide. Big Chocolate is getting rich off this poverty and these problems: Nestlé alone — one company — made $100 billion in sales in 2015, while Ivory Coast and Ghana combined — two entire countries — have a GDP of around $73 billion. All of this in the name of $1 chocolate.

Most of the cocoa that bean-to-bar makers use doesn't come from Africa. They mainly source from Central and South America as well as the Caribbean, areas that historically have higher-quality types of cocoa and higher standards of living. But that doesn't mean everything is hunky-dory there. The issues aren't quite as severe as child slavery in Africa, but cacao farmers everywhere often struggle. One of the biggest problems? They don't always get paid for their beans.

SO HOW MUCH *SHOULD* YOU PAY FOR A BAR OF CHOCOLATE?

Most bean-to-bar chocolate bars these days retail between $8 and $14. Occasionally you'll find some priced lower than this, and often you'll find some priced higher. For example, an Ecuadorian company called To'ak (run by Americans) has released bars that retail for around $300 — and come in a special wooden box with tweezers to allow you to delicately sniff the chocolate's aroma without soiling the square with your fingers.

Still, $14 can still seem like a big investment. However, I'd say that's a pretty low price point to buy the best food of its kind in the world. The best wines retail for hundreds, sometimes thousands, of dollars. Caviar? Forget about it. Spending an average of $10 on a bar that I'll taste over the course of several days or a week seems well worth it to me.

THE FAIR-TRADE FALLACY

WHEN PEOPLE HEAR about the severe problems facing cacao farmers, they generally want to do something — namely, pay farmers more for their hard work. Enter the idea of **fair trade**. Since the 1990s, the concept of fair trade has been the established way to guarantee that your chocolate (or coffee or tea or bananas) is made ethically and, well, fairly.

Here's the rough concept: to get certified as fair-trade suppliers, **farmer co-ops** (farmers who have organized into a group with a governing structure) must meet certain social and environmental standards; then they fill out paperwork and pay a fee to the certifying organization. The big one is Fairtrade Labelling Organizations International, in Germany, but to make it confusing, there's also Fair Trade USA, Fairtrade America, Fair for Life, and others. Once certified, farmers get paid an extra $200 per metric ton of beans for community programs like health care and education. Right now, if a farmer co-op in Ghana isn't Fair Trade USA–certified, they will be able to sell their beans for about $3,168 per metric ton. If they are certified, they'll make that $3,168 per metric ton plus $200 per metric ton to be used toward community programs. If the market price dips low, Fair Trade USA guarantees that farmers will be paid $2,000 per metric ton at a minimum. Chocolate companies pay fair-trade organizations to get certified as well, and then they can sticker their products with a fair-trade label to showcase their commitment.

Sounds easy and fair enough, right?

In reality, fair trade has become a series of boxes that companies can check off, an expensive piece of paper in a long supply chain that often doesn't guarantee that the farmers make any more money, never mind a fair wage. Dandelion Chocolate, for example, chooses not to use fair trade because it costs farmer co-ops quite a bit to get certified and only co-ops (not individual farmers) are eligible. The same can often be said of organic and other certifications. For example, in Tanzania, a co-op will pay $8,000 for a visit from the organic certification auditors.

Farmer co-ops often end up beholden to the organization that covered the cost of the fair-trade paperwork, an organization that may or may not make the co-ops jump through hoops to get any of their money — if they get it at all. Even if they do get some of that money, more of it goes to the fair-trade bureaucracy than to the farmers for their community programs. Beyond that, fair trade only addresses economics, not quality. Under fair-trade principles, poor-quality beans garner the same price as high-quality beans, which doesn't exactly encourage anyone to deliver a good product.

Cacao farmers in the Dominican Republic use long pruning hooks to carefully cut cacao pods from high branches.

Chocolate Pioneers
MOTT GREEN AND THE GRENADA CHOCOLATE COMPANY

SOLAR POWER. SAILBOATS. BICYCLES. And fair wages for all. Mott Green's chocolate company is anything but ordinary. Of course, he was a pretty extraordinary person. Born David Friedman, he grew up on Staten Island and, among other unusual things, lived with homeless anarchists in Philadelphia for most of his 20s, while he worked on projects like bringing electricity to abandoned houses for the homeless and then, in the East Village in New York City, building solar-powered showers for squatters. In the mid-1990s he moved to the Caribbean island country of Grenada — where he'd spent childhood summers with his family while his father, a doctor, treated locals — and lived in a remote hut powered by solar energy. His name, Mott Green, came from the way the locals pronounced his nickname, Moth, and his interest in environmental issues.

Mott started drinking cocoa tea, a Caribbean favorite made with grated cocoa and spices, and quickly became interested in the local cocoa economy. With the help of friend and cofounder Doug Brown, he built all the machinery to open a chocolate factory and in 1999 started the Grenada Chocolate Company as a co-op. All the employees earn the same amount, and the slogan is "tree to bar." The company is special in that it makes fine chocolate right in the place where cacao grows, and the chocolate it makes is fantastic: it's won a slew of awards, and for good reason. The company has also remained a leader in green growing and production practices. For example, in 2012 Mott brought bars to Europe on a sail-powered ship; the bars were then distributed by volunteer cyclists in Amsterdam. Mott called it "the first

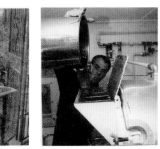

carbon-neutral trans-Atlantic mass chocolate delivery."

Unfortunately, in 2013 disaster struck. While tinkering with a solar-powered machine for cooling chocolate during transport, Mott was electrocuted and died. Despite this tremendous loss, the company has stayed strong. Today it works with farmers on more than 200 acres of farmland and even helps them get organic certification. Grenada Chocolate's commitment to organic farming, environmental sustainability, and fair labor are unparalleled. Plus, it makes some of the best chocolate around.

Devil Dogs

Recipe from Jennifer King, Liddabit Sweets

LEVEL:
Advanced

Yield

30 to 40
dogs

KNOW THIS IS supposed to be a book for grown-ups with refined chocolate recipes, but I have a confession: I love junk food. I bet you do too. That's why I can't get enough of Liddabit Sweets, a Brooklyn–based artisan candy company that makes the most scrumptious versions of your childhood favorites (as well as some crazy-good concoctions of their own creation), all with local, seasonal, responsible ingredients. In other words, they've ditched the high-fructose corn syrup and mass production in favor of high-end chocolate and handcrafted care.

In that case, you really can't call it "junk food": just good, delicious food. This recipe reimagines that childhood favorite, the devil dog, a bone-shaped chocolate cake with white marshmallowy goo in the middle. The cake itself is based on the sour-cream chocolate creation in *Sky High* by Alisa Huntsman and Peter Wynne. Of course, two chocolate cakes weren't enough for Jen: the frosting in the middle is all chocolate too. If you're super serious about chocolate (and who isn't?), try her bonus step of enrobing the entire treat in chocolate. While you should, of course, use good-quality chocolate in every recipe in this book, this is one in which you might not want to use a 2-ounce $17 bar, since the enrobing step calls for 2 pounds of chocolate.

recipe continues on next page

Devil Dogs continued

SOUR-CREAM CHOCOLATE CAKE

2 cups plus 5½ teaspoons sugar

1 cup all-purpose flour

¼ cup Dutch-processed cocoa powder

2 teaspoons baking soda

1 teaspoon fine sea salt

1 cup vegetable oil

1 cup sour cream

2 tablespoons distilled white vinegar

1 teaspoon vanilla extract

2 eggs

CHOCOLATE BUTTERCREAM FROSTING

8 ounces dark chocolate (55 percent cocoa), chopped

¾ cup plus 1½ tablespoons sugar

3 egg whites

6 ounces unsalted butter, cut into 1-inch pieces, at room temperature

SPECIAL EQUIPMENT

Two 13- × 18-inch sheet cake pans, stand mixer (though you can easily substitute a hand mixer if that's all you have)

TO MAKE THE SOUR-CREAM CHOCOLATE CAKE

1. One hour ahead of time, preheat the oven to 350°F (177°C). Grease two 13- × 18-inch sheet cake pans and line them with parchment paper.

2. Sift the sugar, flour, cocoa powder, baking soda, and salt into a large bowl. Stir with a whisk until just combined.

3. In a separate bowl, combine the oil, sour cream, vinegar, and vanilla, and blend until smooth.

4. Pour the wet mixture into the dry mixture and stir gently with the whisk until just barely combined.

5. Whisk the eggs in a small bowl and then add them to the mixture. Stir until they are well blended, making sure there are no lumps or errant clumps of flour.

6. Divide the batter equally between the prepared pans so that it fills them in an even layer, all the way to the corners, if possible.

7. Bake for 20 to 25 minutes, until a tester inserted in the center comes out clean. Let the cakes cool in the pans.

TO MAKE THE CHOCOLATE BUTTERCREAM FROSTING

1. Melt the chocolate in a double boiler or microwave (in short intervals), then set aside to cool slightly.

2. Remove the metal bowl of a stand mixer. Combine the sugar and egg whites in the bowl and set it over a pan of simmering water, like a double boiler setup. Make sure that the bottom of the bowl is not touching the water.

3. Heat, whisking constantly, until the mixture is warm and the sugar is dissolved.

4. Attach the bowl to a stand mixer fitted with the whisk attachment and continue whisking until the mixture is cooled and stiff peaks form, about 7 minutes. (For you pastry nerds, this is called a Swiss meringue.)

5. With the mixer running, add the butter one piece at a time, mixing until each piece is completely incorporated. Continue whisking until a light, fluffy cream forms.

6. Stir in the chocolate until well combined.

ASSEMBLY

1. Remove both cakes from their pans: Run a knife around the edge of the cake and put a cutting board or an unrimmed cookie sheet on top of it. Hold on to the parchment paper and the cutting board as you flip the tray in one swift movement. Peel the parchment paper off both cakes and set one of the cakes in the freezer to chill for 15 minutes.

2. Spread the buttercream onto the second cake so that you have a ½-inch-thick layer of frosting.

3. Remove the first cake from the freezer and lay it on top of the buttercream. Freeze for at least 4 hours and up to overnight.

4. Using a sharp knife, cut the cake into individual-size rectangles. Serve immediately; leftovers will keep for 2 days at room temperature. Or, for an added chocolate bonus, try the variation below.

CHOCOLATE-COVERED DEVIL DOGS

1. After assembling the devil dogs, place them on a wire rack 1 inch apart. Set the rack over a tray. Refrigerate until the cakes are firm.

2. Temper 2 pounds of chocolate (60 to 72 percent cocoa), following the instructions on page 11.

3. Remove the cakes from the refrigerator. Pour the warm chocolate over them, leaving the bottoms uncoated. Let the cakes sit for an hour or so, until the chocolate is fully set; if you're in a hurry to finally eat these delicious treats, place them in the fridge to speed things up. Store any leftovers in the refrigerator, where they will keep for up to 3 days.

WHAT CRAFT MAKERS DO DIFFERENTLY

FOR ALL THE previous stated reasons, fewer and fewer craft chocolate makers go through fair-trade certification these days. Many are adamantly *against* the system and prefer to use a model called **direct trade** (a system in which makers buy ingredients directly from farmers). Rather than rely on a third party to guarantee that farmers are treated fairly, they instead visit farms themselves to see what's happening and what farmers need — and pay them way, way more than even the fair-trade price.

In 2015, for example, the average market price for beans was $3,135.22 per metric ton, but Dandelion Chocolate paid an average of $5,904.51 per metric ton. The least they paid was $4,622.81 per metric ton (for beans from Oko-Caribe in the Dominican Republic; see page 219), and the most they paid was $6,670 per metric ton (for beans from Camino Verde farm in Ecuador; see page 218). That means that on the open market, beans are about $1.42 per pound, while Dandelion paid an average of $2.68. (In the fair-trade

Cacao farmers in Belize slice open cacao pods and remove the pulp and beans.

model, beans average $0.91 to $1.65 per pound, plus $.09 per pound for social projects.) Meanwhile, Art Pollard of Amano Artisan Chocolate has traveled the world to talk with farmers and paid up to $5 per pound for beans. And Maya Mountain, a company in Belize (see page 219), charges up to $14,000 per metric ton for some of its beans, which many makers gladly pay.

It's clear that bean-to-bar makers want to pay farmers fairly for their hard work and their commitment to growing fine-flavor cocoa. "We believe that improving quality is a more sustainable means of increasing the price that producers can charge for their product, and how effectively they can drive more capital into their lives, farms, and community," Dandelion wrote in its 2015 sourcing report. This doesn't mean that they're literally hauling bags of beans on their backs from farm to factory several times a year. Many rely on brokers like Meridian Cacao Company to help them import beans from farmers whom the makers know and have visited.

Taza Chocolate in particular has paved the way for direct trade in chocolate. In 2006 they created an entire direct-trade sourcing program, and in 2010 they started getting an independent third party to verify their claims. That's huge in a world of marketing fluff and buzzwords. Taza visits farmers at least once per year, pays at least $500 per metric ton above the market price, sources high-quality

beans (with strict requirements), requires USDA-certified organic cocoa, and publishes an annual transparency report.

The transparency report has changed the game for the industry, as it reveals exactly what the company pays farmers, numbers that historically have been fudged and fuzzy. Each report also details exactly what happened over the past year at each farm, creating connections among farmer, maker, and consumer that are almost unheard of in this day and age. These connections transcend the dollar amount paid for the cocoa beans, adding a human dimension to the transaction. Other makers have followed Taza's lead, practicing direct trade and releasing transparency reports of their own.

"Direct trade is between human beings, not within a system," said Geoff Watts of Intelligentsia Coffee, which pioneered the model. "A system doesn't have memories. It's codified, a set of ideas, whereas direct trade is all about personal relationships between myself and a farmer where we commit to helping each other." However, that also means that there isn't a formal direct-trade certification system, which can make it tricky to identify a chocolate maker who uses this model.

However, chocolate makers who do use direct trade are usually very open about their methods. And it's not just about dollar amounts. Many makers help farming communities with humanitarian projects; as you'll see in their profile (page 172), Askinosie Chocolate (which is on *Forbes'* list of America's best small companies) goes to great lengths to improve the lives of everyone they meet and work with, and this kind of attention to social justice is spreading across bean-to-bar chocolate.

Beyond sharing 10 percent of their profits with farmers and keeping open books, in Tanzania and the Philippines Askinosie has built wells and schoolhouses, started school lunch programs, and bought textbooks and laptops for kids, among other efforts. Founder Shawn Askinosie visits farmer communities often and works with them on 10-year business plans to help them think about the future and become more self-sufficient. In fact, when he meets with farmers to talk about open books and profit distribution, he requires that all members of the community be present, including women. "We had to come in as a partner, not as a great white savior," Shawn said about his decision to use direct trade to focus on social change.

IS YOUR CHOCOLATE DIRECT TRADE?

THERE ISN'T A FORMAL certification process for direct trade, which means it can be hard to figure out if chocolate makers use that model. Here are a few ways to tell:

1. **THEY NAME THE FARMS.** On the chocolate label, look for information like the farm's name and even sometimes the farmer's name as well as the harvest year. On the maker's website, look for much more detail, such as photos of farms and farmers. The more information, the better.

2. **THEY TALK ABOUT RECENT TRIPS.** Many will tell stories on their websites and social media about past, present, and future trips to visit the farms. Some even offer ways for you to join their trips!

3. **THEY HAVE A GOOD REPUTATION** in the industry. Bean-to-bar chocolate is a small world, and word gets out quickly. Many makers partner together to buy beans, for example, and you'll often see pictures of them together on Facebook or they'll mention one another on their websites. That's usually a good sign that they're using direct trade.

4. **ASK.** Everyone I've ever encountered who practices direct trade is more than willing to talk (sometimes ad nauseum) about their methods.

Chocolate and Churros

**Recipe from Janina O'Leary,
James Beard Award–nominated pastry chef**

LEVEL: *Medium*

Serves
2-3

ONCE UPON A TIME, Spain was the chocolate capital of the world. After all, Spanish conquistadores like Hernán Cortés recognized the dark stuff's power back in the 1500s, and the Spanish were the first to bring it to Europe around that time. But it's been a while.

When I visited Spain a few years ago, though, everyone was still under chocolate's spell, especially when it was served hot and thick alongside churros, traditional Spanish doughnuts. I, of course, joined in wholeheartedly.

For this recipe I called on the queen of doughnuts, pastry chef Janina O'Leary, who has worked at New York City's Per Se and Del Posto, among other places. So go ahead and make these easy at-home churros and dip them in the best sauce ever. Any origin of cocoa should work with these, though nutty and roasty flavor profiles would be particularly great; I recommend trying them all and finding your favorite. I won't judge you if you finish the entire batch every time and drink down any remnants of the irresistible chocolate. Take note that these will only last for about 4 hours — and that's pushing it. In other words, fresh is the name of the churro-and-chocolate game.

CHURROS

- Vegetable oil
- ¼ cup granulated sugar
- 1 teaspoon ground cinnamon
- 1 cup water
- ⅓ cup butter, softened
- 1½ tablespoons brown sugar
- ½ teaspoon salt
- 1 cup all-purpose flour, sifted
- 2 eggs
- ½ teaspoon vanilla extract

MEXICAN CHOCOLATE SAUCE

- ½ cup heavy cream
- ¾ cup chopped chocolate (66 to 70 percent cocoa)
- ½ teaspoon ancho chile powder
- ½ teaspoon vanilla extract
- ¼ teaspoon ground cinnamon

SPECIAL EQUIPMENT

Pastry bag (for a DIY version, see Chef's Tips, page 60) and large star tip

recipe continues on next page

Chocolate and Churros

1. Preheat 1½ to 2 inches of vegetable oil in a 10- to 12-inch frying pan to 375°F (191°C).

2. Stir the granulated sugar and cinnamon together in a dish, then pour the mixture onto a baking sheet and set aside.

3. Combine the water, butter, brown sugar, and salt in a 3-quart saucepan and heat to a good boil. Pour into a large bowl (use your stand mixer's bowl, if you have one). Add the flour and, with the stand mixer or a hand mixer, mix until well blended.

4. In a separate bowl, beat the eggs and vanilla together and then add them to the flour mixture. Stir until the dough is shiny and homogenous.

5. Fill your pastry bag with the dough and attach the largest star tip you have.

6. Test the oil by placing a small amount of dough into it. The dough should bubble up right away. If it doesn't, that means the oil is not hot enough and your churros will turn out soggy. Make sure the oil is at 375°F (191°C).

7. Use the pastry bag to squeeze about a 4-inch length of dough into the oil. Use a small offset spatula to release the dough from the decorator tip, being careful not to burn yourself. Repeat until you have about four churros in the pan, making sure not to crowd the pan.

8. Deep-fry until the churros are golden-brown and cooked through. If the churros brown but are still raw inside, the oil is too hot; pour more oil into the pan and try another batch. If they cook through but don't brown on the outside, the oil is not hot enough; wait a bit for it to heat up before trying again.

9. As the churros finish frying, pull them out of the oil with tongs, place them on a wire rack for a moment to drain, then move them directly onto the baking sheet with the cinnamon sugar and roll them around to coat. Finally, move them to a second wire rack to cool.

10. When the last batch of churros is close to finished, make the chocolate sauce: Heat the heavy cream in a saucepan. Add the chopped chocolate, ancho chile powder, vanilla, and cinnamon, and heat, stirring constantly, until the chocolate is fully melted and the ingredients are thoroughly combined.

11. Pour the chocolate sauce into a small bowl and place the churros on a serving platter. Dip the churros into the chocolate bite by bite, and enjoy!

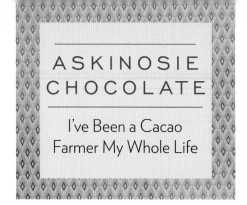

ASKINOSIE CHOCOLATE

I've Been a Cacao Farmer My Whole Life

By Livingston Mwakipesile, as told to Megan Giller on May 29, 2015. Translated from the original Swahili by Kellen Msseemmaa.

Shawn Askinosie talks about fermentation with farmers in Tanzania.

African farmers rarely get to speak for themselves. As Daudi Msseemmaa, the Africa field operations director for Convoy of Hope, which works closely with award-winning Askinosie Chocolate, told me, "Africans are sometimes used as props in the story about what Americans are doing in Africa. I don't think it's intentional. But it's something that naturally happens." That's why this maker profile is different from the others in this book. I don't want to tell a story about Shawn Askinosie. Instead, travel with me to Tanzania to hear a cacao farmer named Livingston Mwakipesile speak for himself about cacao, international trade, and how his life has changed in the past few years because of the bean-to-bar chocolate movement.

WHEN I WAS A LITTLE BOY, I shared a bed with my brother. We were hungry almost all the time, and my parents were mere cacao farmers and didn't have a good life. It's funny to remember now that I'm 64 and my life has changed so much.

Now I own four houses, three of which I rent, and I'm building another one! I didn't go to school until I was 14 because I had to help my parents in the cacao fields, and I only stayed for three years, until what you Americans would call fourth grade. But my children go to the best schools in Mababu. In the evenings and on the weekends I let them study instead of helping me on the plantation, because I don't want them to get used to the cacao plantation. I want them to go to school! They're proud of what their father has done with his life, so they want to study hard and be cacao farmers too. I'd love for one of them to become

Livingston Mwakipesile

an accountant so that when our little cacao co-op grows into a big company, he can do the financials.

Now I own three cows and some chickens, so we eat eggs almost every day, which is unusual here. My wife grows vegetables, and we eat those too. My favorite thing to eat is rice and beef, but I don't eat too much beef because it's expensive. And chocolate? We almost never eat chocolate, even though we grow cacao for a living. I had never even tried it until Shawnie brought some back to Mababu last year. It was tasty!

I remember the first time I saw Shawnie. It was in 2013, and I was immediately happy, because I could tell he was interested in working with us cacao farmers, and I was sure he'd be able to sell our beans. Before I met him, we weren't sure if we'd be able to sell the beans for a good price, or even at all. We always had a good crop, but often we couldn't find a good buyer and would have to sell them at such low prices that we could barely make a profit. We would often go hungry.

But Shawnie changed all of that. He has particular requirements for how we grow and ferment the cacao beans, but he buys them for much more than anyone else, and he gives us 10 percent of the profits. I could just take my 10 percent, but all of the farmers in the Mababu CCF co-op have decided to keep it in the group. Anyone in the group can buy shares and borrow from the group.

Shawnie used to be a lawyer, and now he comes once a year and teaches us strategies to achieve our goals. It makes me feel like a young man again. We talk in present tense about our goals, like they have already happened. The first time, one of the men said, "I woke up this

continued on next page

morning and I had a mattress, and I looked up and I had a ceiling in my house. My wife was so happy because she was able to go to the store and buy what she wanted at the market." Tears were streaming down his face.

Shawnie has helped our community in other ways too. He helped build three classrooms, so instead of studying under a tree in the rainy season, the children can study in a classroom. The students now have textbooks and laptops. For a long time Mababu children starved, and the girls dropped out of school to sell themselves in exchange for food. Shawnie heard about this when he first came to our country. We grow the most wonderful rice in Mababu, and he sells it in the United States and gives us 100 percent of the profit, for school lunches. The headmaster of the school tells us that there have been no unwanted pregnancies since Shawnie started the program.

Because of Shawnie, my family has expanded our plantation. It's on four acres, and now we are growing more cacao beans than Shawnie can even afford to buy. I hope Askinosie Chocolate will expand so he can buy all of my beans. There are other small companies and middlemen that will buy them, but I wish Askinosie could buy them all or help us find a buyer, because the other people pay us such a small price.

I would love to travel someday. I'd come to the United States so I could see how things are different from where I live.

Livingston's wife, Mama Mpoki, on Askinosie's label (above) and holding cacao pods (below)

Budino di Cioccolato

Recipe from Marea

LEVEL: *Medium*

Serves

◇ 12 ◇

RECENTLY HAD DINNER at Marea, an Italian seafood restaurant in New York City, and the dessert stole the show. Now, this happens relatively often to me, since I'm a complete fiend for sweets, especially chocolate (duh). But this was different. Pastry chef Francis Joven paired a rich chocolate *budino* (Italian pudding) with bright pomegranate seeds and fresh tarragon, a combination I'd never tasted before. I was hooked!

Here, for your eating pleasure, is an at-home version of this upscale dessert. I particularly like the sablé cookie crumbles. Sablés are French salted butter cookies, and they're light and delicious and provide a fun crunch in addition to the fresh pomegranate seeds in the composed dessert. It looks complicated, but really there are just a bunch of (pretty easy) steps. It will take you about 2 hours' active time to make this recipe, though there's a lot of waiting around. You can use a single-origin chocolate in this recipe, but it might be eclipsed by the other flavors like fresh herbs.

SPECIAL EQUIPMENT
12 three-inch ring molds, stand mixer (though you can easily substitute a hand mixer if that's all you have)

recipe continues on next page

Budino di Cioccolato continued

CHOCOLATE GANACHE

- 1 cup heavy cream
- ½ cup whole milk
- 7 ounces dark chocolate (70 percent cocoa), chopped

1. Combine the cream and milk in a saucepan and heat to a simmer.

2. Add the chocolate and, using a whisk or spatula, blend until smooth.

3. Divide the ganache among 12 small (3-inch) ring molds. Freeze for at least 4 hours but preferably overnight.

OLIVE OIL SABLÉ COOKIE CRUMBLE

- ¾ cup (1½ sticks) butter, at room temperature
- ¾ cup sugar
- 4 egg yolks
- ¼ cup extra-virgin olive oil
- ⅔ teaspoon baking powder
- Pinch of salt
- 1⅓ cups all-purpose flour

1. In a stand mixer fitted with the paddle attachment, cream the butter and sugar.

2. Set out the remaining ingredients, measured as needed, combining the baking powder and salt into one bowl, next to the stand mixer, so you'll be able to keep the mixer running and easily add ingredients.

3. Add the egg yolks and stir to mix, then drizzle in the oil and stir to mix, using a spatula to scrape down the sides of the bowl. Add the baking powder and salt and stir to mix.

4. Add the flour and, using a spatula, stir by hand until just barely incorporated. Make sure to scrape down the sides of the bowl.

5. Lay a big piece of parchment paper on a clean, flat surface. Place the dough in the middle of the paper and cover it with a sheet of plastic wrap. Using a rolling pin, flatten the dough evenly until it is about ¼ to ½ inch thick. Remove the plastic wrap and transfer the parchment paper and dough to a baking sheet. Use a fork to prick the dough all over (this will allow steam to escape and keep the dough from rising). Refrigerate or freeze until very firm, at least several hours.

6. Preheat the oven to 325°F (163°C).

7. Bake the dough for about 10 minutes, until golden brown. Let cool completely.

8. Using a rolling pin, crumble the cookie into small pieces.

CHOCOLATE GLAZE

- ⅔ cup heavy cream
- ⅓ cup water
- 3⅓ tablespoons sugar
- 8¾ ounces dark chocolate (70 percent cocoa), chopped

1. Combine the cream, water, and sugar in a small saucepan and bring to a boil.

2. Place the chocolate in a big bowl. Pour the cream mixture over the chocolate and let sit for a minute or two.

3. Stir with a spatula using a circular motion, starting in the center and working your way out, until the ingredients are fully blended. The glaze should be super shiny.

ASSEMBLY

- Ganache (see above)
- Chocolate glaze (see above)
- Olive oil sablé cookie crumble (see above)
- 6 tablespoons cocoa nibs
- ¾ cup pomegranate seeds
- 3 tablespoons chopped fresh tarragon
- Few pinches of sea salt

1. Remove the ring molds from the freezer. Using your hands to warm them, carefully slide the molds off the ganache and place on individual plates.

2. If the chocolate glaze has cooled, warm it in the microwave in 30-second increments until liquid. Pour over the frozen ganache. Place in the refrigerator until you're ready to serve.

3. When you're ready to serve, pull the plates out of the refrigerator and let them sit at room temperature for 5 to 10 minutes. Garnish each plate with the olive oil sablé cookie crumble, cocoa nibs, 1 tablespoon pomegranate seeds, fresh tarragon, and a pinch of sea salt.

CHAPTER SEVEN

THE FUTURE
— of —
CHOCOLATE

THERE WERE ONLY a handful of bean-to-bar makers in the country in 2005. Now there are around 200, and the number is growing every day. John Nanci, the founder of Chocolate Alchemy, estimates that for every company we know, there are two or three more people making chocolate in their basement, waiting to come to market. In other words, it's the golden years of good chocolate.

CRAFT CHOCOLATE GROWS UP

MANY EXPERTS BELIEVE that we'll eventually reach a critical mass of bean-to-bar makers, at which point only the truly remarkable will survive: those using special beans who have mastered not only the chocolate-making process but also marketing.

Here's what some of the best makers are doing to stand out from the pack.

Flavored and Inclusion Bars

"The successful bean-to-bar chocolate makers don't make a product that they're enamored with themselves," Alex Whitmore, the founder and CEO of Taza, explained. "They make what the consumer wants. I'd love to make beautiful single-origin bars," he continued. "But single-origin Madagascar chocolate bars don't sell. If you want to go nationwide, you need to be selling flavored bars." Think blends as well as inclusions like dried raspberries (see page 71 for a rundown of the craziest inclusions).

100 Percent Bars

Several makers told me they created a 100 percent cocoa bar (a bar with absolutely no other ingredients besides cocoa, not even sugar) originally just as an experiment. But the intense chocolate has caught on. True aficionados love it for the cred it brings as well as the way it

highlights unique flavor notes, and the paleo/CrossFit world loves it for having an abundance of antioxidants and no sugar, while still tasting truly of chocolate. Expect to see more and more of these guys.

Confections and Baked Goods

As much as I love a good bar of chocolate, I can also dig into a box of bonbons or a brownie. American makers are figuring out that these sweet treats make up a huge market, and they're creating delicious treats using bean-to-bar chocolate. Think Fruition's corn nuts coated in dark chocolate and dusted with jalapeño, French Broad's sorghum caramel truffle, and Dandelion's brownie flight (see page 67 for the recipe).

Meanwhile, candy makers like Philadelphia's Shane Confectionery, the oldest continuously run candy shop in the country, have also started to make chocolate from scratch. The store began making bean-to-bar chocolate in 2014 to educate consumers and help them develop an appreciation for fine-flavor cocoa. They plan to make all of the chocolate for their confections from scratch and at some point will even release house-made bars. This is just one example of how the bean-to-bar market continues to expand.

Baking Chocolate

Hello, chocolate chips, cocoa nibs, cocoa powder, and big ol' quantities of bean-to-bar chocolate sold in bulk. High-end restaurants are moving toward using American-made chocolate (Chez Panisse, for example, uses Amano), and now consumers can get their hands on it for baking as well (see the list of places to buy bean-to-bar baking chocolate on page 217).

Collaboration

Almost every chocolate maker I talk to likes to quote JFK: "A rising tide lifts all boats." These folks travel across the world to learn more about chocolate, buy beans together, and troubleshoot chocolate-making problems together. For example, it's pretty normal for aspiring chocolate makers to call up Dandelion, in San Francisco, to ask for advice. This kind of camaraderie will only grow.

$10 Is Normal

In chapter 6 I talked about why cheap chocolate hurts everyone. Consumers are starting to accept the higher price tag for chocolate, as well as the idea that it's a luxury item like wine. In the coming years we'll see a greater acceptance of that fact, as well as climbing prices for fantastic bars.

THE CHOCOLATE GARAGE

MANY SPECIALTY STORES buy a solid selection of chocolate bars and call it a day, but The Chocolate Garage, in Palo Alto, California, goes much further. Owner Sunita de Tourreil crowdfunds small-batch bars from a handful of makers like Areté, Castronovo, Lonohana, Patric, and Rogue and even finds private lenders in special cases. Sometimes customers wait over a year to get the chocolate they invested in, while the artisan maker buys beans, figures out the best way to make chocolate from them, and crafts an exquisite bar. In other words, Sunita has created an entire community of people engaged in *making* the chocolate, not just buying and eating it. If you're lucky enough to find yourself in Palo Alto on a Saturday morning or Wednesday evening (the only hours the Garage is open), stop by for a tasting and say hello.

MICHAEL LAISKONIS AND THE INSTITUTE OF CULINARY EDUCATION

ASK MOST PASTRY CHEFS where chocolate comes from, and they'll point to a bag of Valrhona. *But, like, before that? I don't know. A plant or something.*

Professional pastry schools barely include more than an introductory lecture on how chocolate is made. But one school wants to change that. In 2015, the Institute of Culinary Education opened the Chocolate Lab, an impressive educational bean-to-bar facility, with lauded pastry chef Michael Laiskonis at its helm. It immediately started filling up classes left and right. What makes ICE's program interesting is that it's tailored to pastry chefs, not people who want to start their own companies making chocolate. This will change the face of pastry, since presumably when people know where an ingredient comes from and how to make it, they'll understand how to work with it even better. Michael even has "playdates" with other pastry chefs, like superstar Johnny Iuzzini, who is opening his own bean-to-bar company in upstate New York soon.

But the most exciting part to me is that Michael is discovering, cataloging, and sharing information that big companies like Mars and Hershey have known for years and kept locked down. For example, what happens when you age chocolate, and how exactly do you make Dutch-processed cocoa? In other words, he's craft chocolate's big data scientist.

Chocolate Sorbet

Recipe from Guittard Chocolate

LEVEL:
Easy

Yield

3 cups

SIMPLE, SWEET, AND DELICIOUS are three good words to describe this recipe. That makes sense, since it's from Guittard Chocolate, one of my favorite old-school all-American companies, based in San Francisco. (Read more about them on page 111.) As Amy Guittard, the fifth generation of the family to help run the company, says, sometimes we assume sorbet is a light dessert, but with this recipe, that's far from the case. It's intense in its richness, and since it's water-based, it will let all the flavor notes of your favorite bar of chocolate shine, whether it's single origin or a blend. If you want to be extra fancy, serve with chocolate curls or cocoa nibs as a garnish.

2¼ cups water

¾ cup plus 1½ tablespoons sugar

⅓ cup natural cocoa powder (not Dutch-processed), sifted

½ teaspoon salt

4½ ounces chocolate (70 percent cocoa), chopped finely

½ teaspoon vanilla extract

SPECIAL EQUIPMENT
Ice cream maker (though you can make do without one)

1. Pour 1½ cups of the water into a large saucepan and whisk in the sugar, cocoa powder, and salt. Bring to a boil and let boil for exactly 45 seconds, whisking continuously. Remove the mixture from the heat.

2. Add the chocolate and stir until it's melted. Then stir in the vanilla and the remaining ¾ cup water.

3. Chill the mixture thoroughly in the refrigerator, for at least 12 hours and up to 24 hours, to let the flavors meld.

4. Remove from the refrigerator. Using a whisk, blend the mixture gently. Strain into a second bowl.

5. Freeze the sorbet in your ice cream maker according to the manufacturer's instructions. If you don't have an ice cream maker, put the sorbet in a large bowl in the freezer and stir every hour for the first 3 hours, then let it sit for 24 hours, until frozen, before serving. Store in an airtight container in the freezer, where the sorbet will keep for up to 2 months.

CHOCOLATE IS FOR EVERYBODY

THERE'S ONE TREND that's not moving fast enough, and that's craft chocolate being made by all sorts of people, including women and minorities. Out of the 200 or so American chocolate companies, about 32 are owned by women and 3 by African Americans. In the history of the Good Food Awards, as of 2016, only one solely female-owned bean-to-bar chocolate company has won an award (Acalli), and no minority-owned bean-to-bar chocolate company has ever won anything. Meanwhile, out of the roughly 30 American bean-to-bar companies who've won awards at the International Chocolate Awards, only one was owned solely by a woman (Castronovo), and none were owned by minorities.

Fifteen years ago, though, there were no minority makers at all, just five or so white dudes making craft chocolate. In other words, things are changing, albeit slowly. That's why I'm calling this section "Chocolate Is for Everybody," a play on feminist bell hooks's important book *Feminism Is for Everybody*. Hooks believes that feminism, rather than being strictly about gender equality, is about equality for all people. Similarly, I believe craft chocolate is about more than chocolate; it's about raising our ethical standards for all food and taking into account everyone along the supply chain as well as increasing diversity along that supply chain.

Why is this even an issue? I asked female chocolate makers why they think there aren't more women making chocolate from scratch. Many cited how physically demanding the job is — hauling heavy bags of beans, standing for 10 to 15 hours at a time, fixing machines. Oh yeah, machines. Working with them can be daunting. "As women we aren't socialized to question how things work in the way that men are," Caitlin Lacey, Dandelion's production manager, told me recently. She said that working with machines to make chocolate "was a big hurdle" for her, something she'd always been scared of. She learned how to approach them, though, and triumphed.

"It's affected my personal life as well," she continued. "If something breaks at my house, I'm much more willing to try to fix it than I would have been before, rather than call my dad or boyfriend. I haven't made great strides, but instead of having a moment where I shut off when it's broken and I need someone else to help me, I try to do more myself."

Minorities aren't represented well in the bean-to-bar world either, especially African Americans. "Startup capital is an issue for all minority businesses," Dominic Maloney of Sol Cacao, a Harlem-based company that he runs with his two brothers, explained. He and his brothers emigrated to the United States from Trinidad when they were young, and he said that other Caribbean immigrants are flabbergasted when he tells them they make chocolate themselves. They see cacao as a crop to be exported to Belgium or Switzerland, not an ingredient that they could work with themselves. The brothers want to inspire Caribbean people to make chocolate. Dominic said that he sees craft chocolate as a "medium to inform the local community about the importance of reading nutritional labels and health benefits" as diabetes ravages the country, especially African-American communities.

Meanwhile, Journey Shannon, an African-American female chocolate maker who owns Noir d'Ebene in Evanston, Illinois, said that she thinks there might be so few African Americans making bean-to-bar chocolate because of the stigma of working in a kitchen; for some, making food means following in Mammy's footsteps more than Escoffier's. She doesn't believe that being African American or female has helped or hurt her in this industry. "I'm a black woman, I'm a chocolatier," she said. "But am I good? If I don't have a good product, it's irrelevant." Yet those qualifiers don't bother her. "We differentiate each other by our race, our hair color, our

Nicholas, Daniel, and Dominic Maloney of Sol Cacao make bean-to-bar chocolate in Harlem.

size. Whatever gets me out there, I'm okay with it," she said. "We're not mature enough yet to identify each other as humans."

As more bean-to-bar chocolate companies come to market and as people get used to the idea that chocolate is more than candy, I suspect that we'll see more and more types of people start making it, which can only benefit the world of chocolate. Because, after all, chocolate is for everybody.

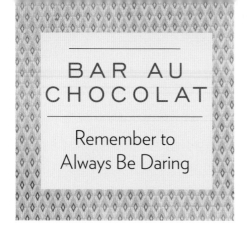

BAR AU CHOCOLAT

Remember to Always Be Daring

NICOLE TRUTANICH makes great chocolate, and she also happens to be a woman. That's unusual in a field dominated by men. But why should a story about a chocolate maker who is female become a story about a Female Chocolate Maker?

After all, Nicole's chocolate can stand on its own, without any backstory. Bar Au Chocolat, her Los Angeles–based brand, won five awards at the 2015 Academy of Chocolate, including a gold medal. She's been featured at events at the Chocolate Garage in Palo Alto, a stamp of approval in this industry, and the beloved West Coast ice cream shop Salt & Straw has used her chocolate in their ice cream.

Yet when I talked to Nicole recently, she told me that the number one question she gets is, Why aren't there more female chocolate makers? It's true that they're a rare breed. I

can list the number of well-known stand-alone female chocolate makers on one hand: Acalli, Cacao Atlanta, Castronovo, Ethereal. "I just wish I weren't called a 'woman chocolate maker,'" Nicole told me. "I wish I were just one of them."

After all, there are other reasons that Nicole stands out besides her gender. The first? She's taking her time. Fifteen years ago there were maybe five bean-to-bar chocolate makers in the country; as the number has increased, many have begun rushing to market with sub-par bars in order to capitalize on the trend.

Nicole, on the other hand, moves almost painstakingly slowly. When she started making chocolate in 2010, she peeled each roasted bean by hand. She sources gorgeous paper to package her bars and uses intricate Japanese folding methods to wrap them (which, for rubes like me, makes them almost impossible to rewrap; I often end up crudely crumpling the paper around the remaining chocolate).

She's cherry-picked a few specialty stores to carry her brand and doesn't want to promote herself until she's absolutely ready. "There's plenty of time to market and do PR," she said. "I focus on trying to make delicious chocolate."

For many bean-to-bar makers, chocolate is the beginning and end of the story. But Nicole wants to be different. She wants to stay "niche" with her chocolate and make other products to appeal to a larger audience and run a successful business — such as her Culinary Traditions series, foods that live up to the Bar Au Chocolat standards but aren't necessarily, well, bars. Think local dried persimmons, cocoa nib granola,

pulse

house blend dark chocolate 70%
aged in coffee beans

BAR AU CHOCOLAT

✳

day of the dead | día de los muertos
november 2016

net weight 2.1 oz | 60 g

Here's how Nicole describes the experience she wants her customers to have:

Chocolate is a sensual experience. I wanted my packaging to reflect this. I thought about the texture of the paper, the fold, the anticipation of unwrapping a bar, the aroma as you take it out of the copper foil, the simplicity of the bar design, and finally the tasting of the chocolate. I wanted to create an artistic, authentic, distinctive, delicious, and inspired tasting experience. I wanted the act of unwrapping my bar to be sensual and intimate. In the end, I want people to feel the pulse and passion behind my chocolate.

shortbread with roasted cocoa nibs. You can find them all, as well as "cocoa-inspired sweets and savories" like hot chocolate, pastries, coffee, ice cream, and more, at her café and storefront in Manhattan Beach, California, called Bar Au Chocolat Atelier.

Making chocolate is an unusual career change for a late-40-something who spent almost 20 years in advertising, and her business model reveals an even more unusual attitude for someone from the advertising world. Then again, Nicole seems to live by the Latin aphorism on Bar Au Chocolat's labels, *memento avdere semper*: "remember to always be daring."

Pop Rocks Chocolate Bark

Recipe from Sebastián Cisneros, Cocanú Chocolate

LEVEL:
Medium

Yield

Approximately
1 pound

KNOW WHAT YOU'RE THINKING. Pop Rocks? In a book on *high-end* chocolate? Absolutely! The fun punch of Pop Rocks adds an extra element to this chocolate bark, making an irresistible treat. For the uninitiated, chocolate bark is a sheet of solid chocolate covered in nuts, dried fruit, or whatever you'd like, broken into bite-size pieces for you to munch on. This recipe mixes the extra ingredients right into the bark. It comes from Cocanú Chocolate in Portland, Oregon, a bean-to-bar maker that deviates from the single-origin norm by including ingredients like bee pollen, fernet, and Palo Santo wood. Founder Sebastián Cisneros calls this Pop Rocks and cocoa nibs bar Moonwalk, and there's definitely an astronaut quality to the whole thing. Sebastián suggests using bright Madagascar chocolate and cocoa nibs, because the high acidity cuts the sweetness of the Pop Rocks. You can find roasted cocoa nibs from many bean-to-bar makers these days. Pop Rocks, on the other hand, can be tricky to find in grocery stores; online is probably your best bet.

Chocolate bark is a fun trick to have in your bag, and it's definitely a way to add some creativity to your chocolate repertoire. Try substituting the Pop Rocks and cocoa nibs in this recipe with your favorite inclusions: almonds, dried cherries, anything.

recipe continues on next page

14 ounces dark chocolate
(at least 60 percent
cocoa), chopped

1¾ ounces roasted
cocoa nibs

4 packs Pop Rocks
(38 grams total)

SPECIAL EQUIPMENT
6- x 8-inch sheet pan

Pop Rocks Chocolate Bark
continued

1. Temper the chocolate, following the instructions on page 11.

2. Line a 6- × 8-inch sheet pan with parchment paper.

3. Mix the cocoa nibs and Pop Rocks into the tempered chocolate.

4. Pour the mixture onto the baking sheet and spread it around with a spatula.

5. Transfer to the refrigerator and let cool for 20 minutes.

6. Once the chocolate is solid, peel off the parchment paper and break the chocolate into smaller portions. You can store the bark in an airtight container at room temperature, where it will keep for up to 2 weeks. Or, if you're like me, just eat it immediately.

CHEF'S TIP

If you're having trouble finding a sheet pan so small, try a pan from your toaster oven. Or, if you're in dire straits, you can pour the mixture on a larger sheet, taking care not to let it spread to the edges. The resulting bark might be a bit thinner, but it will still taste good.

UNTEMPERED CHOCOLATE BARK
You don't technically have to temper chocolate to make bark. If you don't, you'll have to store the resulting bark in the freezer, to keep it from blooming, and then let it warm to room temperature piece by piece as you eat it. But if that doesn't bother you, here's how to do it: Rather than tempering the chocolate, simply melt it in a double boiler or microwave (see page 10 for detailed instructions). Then follow the directions above, adding the mix-ins, pouring evenly over a baking sheet lined with parchment paper, letting cool in the refrigerator, and then transferring to the freezer (see Chef's Tips, page 60).

DANDELION

Big in Japan

IT WAS A FAMILIAR SCENE: Silicon Valley, two nerds, a garage, machinery, and electronics. Only these particular two nerds weren't working on retooling a motherboard or creating an app. Todd Masonis and Cameron Ring were huddled over a hair dryer, blasting cocoa shells away from nibs. On a nearby table sat a tiny coffee roaster and a half-destroyed tempering machine. They were making chocolate.

Straight out of college at Stanford, the two had started a tech company called Plaxo with Sean Parker (whom you might remember from Napster), and in 2008, after a few tough years, they sold it to Comcast for upwards of $150 million. That left them with

plenty of time on their hands. So what did they do? Started making chocolate, of course. "We were used to writing software," Todd remembered, "but building a machine that could do something physical was new and interesting." The two Stanford grads harnessed their tech startup know-how and applied it to a new field. They wouldn't be artists creating a masterpiece but instead pragmatists solving a problem: how to make the best chocolate possible. Through rigorous methodology, they've now gotten it down to a science, which means that after they experiment to find the right combinations for a particular bean, any Dandelion Chocolate employee can make the perfect chocolate bar. Right now the company employs between 10 and 15 chocolate makers, a vastly different model from other artisan companies, where the sole chocolate maker is viewed as an artist.

Now they're taking that model even further, expanding into a giant factory a few blocks away from the original one on Valencia Street in San Francisco's Mission District. They're keeping the current spot as a café, an education facility, and a place to make special-edition bars, but most production will happen in the new space. Ten times the amount of production, in fact. "It's not good enough to double the amount or eke out 10 percent or 20 percent more," Todd explained about the economics of scale. "We have to get to a whole new order of magnitude."

The team has done 10 times more work to get to that new order of magnitude as well. They sent a team to Italy to try different machines.

continued on next page

Todd Masonis (left); Dandelion's café and factory in San Francisco (right)

DANDELION continued

They went to Colorado to visit Steve DeVries, the father of the American movement, to compare his antique machinery to newer machines and then buy some of those superior antiques. "We tested the exact same beans from three different processes to try to figure out which machinery was used on the beans at each factory" and which worked the best, Todd said.

"For every machine that we get, we do taste tests and validate and say we won't do this unless it makes chocolate that's better than what we do today."

The expansion can't come quickly enough. For years Dandelion has had scaling problems. For over a year they couldn't fill wholesale orders and had more than 500 stores across the country on their waiting list. Their wholesale manager often said her job description was "customer disappointment management," because she turned people away all day. (It was like that even in the beginning: "We had to ration the bars," Todd said about their first Christmas in production, in 2012. "We told people, 'You cannot buy more than five chocolate bars per day, because it's not fair to everyone else.' So people would come with their friends, who would buy the bars, or they would try to trick us.")

That kind of demand extends outside the country too. In 2016 Dandelion opened a location in Tokyo. Eager Japanese chocolate lovers waited for hours for the store to open, in a line that wound around the block. Bars and pastries sold out immediately that day, and have every day since. Remarkably, some bars in that Tokyo facility are made on-site, meaning Dandelion has figured out a way to translate its chocolate-making know-how halfway around the world.

Japan has such a big appetite for bean-to-bar chocolate that Dandelion has opened two more cafés, one near the shrine at Ise Jingu. In other words, come for the sun goddess, stay for the chocolate.

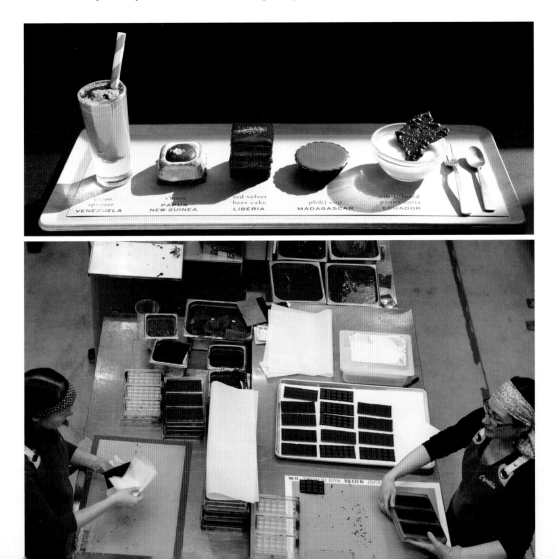

cacao
spritzer
VENEZUELA

s'more
PAPUA
NEW GUINEA

red velvet
beet cake
LIBERIA

pb&j cup
MADAGASCAR

nib-infused
panna cotta
ECUADOR

THE REST OF THE WORLD LOVES CHOCOLATE

THESE DAYS YOU'LL FIND American-style bean-to-bar chocolate in far-flung regions way outside America. Canada and Great Britain are catching up, as are the rest of Europe, Australia, and New Zealand. Asia is also developing a taste for chocolate; some of it might be green tea Kit Kats, but you'll also find a ton of craft chocolate lovers. Japan in particular is smitten with bean-to-bar chocolate. Dozens of local companies are launching there, and in 2016 Dandelion opened its first Asian location, outside Tokyo. India has started to produce cocoa and craft chocolate as well, though frankly I haven't seen anything great from that area yet. But with all the interest, I expect that to change relatively soon.

In other words, so much chocolate, so little stomach space. If you have to narrow it down, here are 14 of my favorite bean-to-bar makers outside the United States:

AKESSON'S
(United Kingdom)

AMEDEI
(Italy)

CACAOSUYO
(Peru)

CHOCOLATE NAIVE
(Lithuania)

DOMORI
(Italy)

FRIIS-HOLM
(Denmark)

GRENADA CHOCOLATE COMPANY
(Grenada)

MAROU
(Vietnam)

PRALUS
(France)

PUMP STREET
(United Kingdom)

RÓZSAVÖLGYI CSOKOLÁDÉ
(Hungary)

SMOOTH CHOCOLATOR
(Australia)

SOMA
(Canada)

VALRHONA
(France)

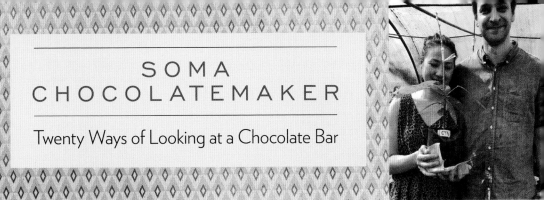

SOMA CHOCOLATEMAKER

Twenty Ways of Looking at a Chocolate Bar

FLOURLESS FUDGE CAKE. Whiskey-chocolate gelato. Preserved plum truffles. Gianduja drinking chocolate. Walk into one of Soma's shops in Toronto and you may never leave, because David Castellan and Cynthia Leung aren't your average bean-to-bar makers. Their imaginations run wild with possibilities for chocolate, which has led them to make much more than award-winning bars; they've created a paradise for chocolate lovers of all sorts. Starting in 2003, the couple was one of the first in North America to make chocolate from scratch, and they have taken a different tack than most, creating delicious confections and baked goods as well as award-winning chocolate bars that, at one event I held, practically forced a stampede. "Wherever we go," Cynthia told me, "our brains are wired to wonder, 'Can we do that in chocolate?'"

Triple Chocolate Chunk Cookies

Recipe from Miro Uskokovic, pastry chef at Gramercy Tavern and Untitled at the Whitney

LEVEL:
Easy

Yield

About
4 dozen
large cookies

LUCKED INTO an event a few years ago where Miro Uskokovic was serving piles of these ultimate chocolate chip cookies. I must have eaten about 10, and I snuck another couple home (no judgment!). Since then I've visited Untitled at the Whitney (the museum's restaurant) over and over, for cookies as much as art.

You'd never know it, but Miro uses Thomas Keller's brand of gluten-free flour for his version of these cookies. (It's called Cup4Cup, and you can buy it from Amazon, among other places.) He says he originally tried the gluten-free flour to have the option but liked it so well that he stuck with it. The recipe works with regular all-purpose flour too. Miro recommends Kerrygold butter and Guittard baking chocolate wafers in particular. I like that idea, because while the recipe benefits from high-quality chocolate, you don't need to use single-origin chocolate in this one. One of my other favorite parts about it is that it showcases three types of chocolate — dark, milk, and white — and how they play off one another to make what the New York media call the best chocolate chip cookie in the city.

1½ cups (3 sticks) unsalted butter, at room temperature

1½ cups light brown sugar

1 cup plus 2 tablespoons granulated sugar

1 tablespoon vanilla extract

1 teaspoon kosher salt

3 eggs

2 egg yolks

4 cups all-purpose flour

1 teaspoon baking soda

2¼ cups dark chocolate chunks (72 percent cocoa)

1½ cups milk chocolate chunks

1 cup white chocolate chunks

Sea salt, for garnish

SPECIAL EQUIPMENT
Stand mixer (though you can easily substitute a hand mixer if that's all you have)

recipe continues on next page

Triple Chocolate Chunk Cookies

continued

1. In a stand mixer fitted with the whisk attachment, combine the butter, brown sugar, granulated sugar, vanilla, and kosher salt. Mix at low speed for 30 seconds.

2. Add the eggs and egg yolks and mix at medium speed until the mixture resembles thick frosting, 5 to 8 minutes. You should see the contents double in size and get lighter and fluffier.

3. In a second bowl, sift together the flour and baking soda.

4. Switch the mixer attachment from whisk to paddle. Add the flour and baking soda and mix until just barely incorporated.

5. Add the chocolate chunks and mix to combine at slow speed or by hand.

6. Transfer the dough to an airtight container and put it in the fridge to rest overnight. If you're short on time, you can pull it out of the fridge after 2 to 4 hours.

7. Remove the dough from the fridge and let it come to room temperature. Preheat the oven to 375°F (191°C).

8. Using an ice cream scoop, scoop evenly sized balls of dough (roughly 2 tablespoons each) onto an ungreased baking sheet, making sure to leave a few inches of room around each. Sprinkle each cookie with a pinch of sea salt. Bake for 8 to 9 minutes, or until the edges are golden brown and the cookie is still soft inside. Let cool (almost) completely.

9. Eat while slightly warm, with a glass of cold whole milk!

Chocolate Revolution

I FOUND MYSELF back in Portland in the middle of a heat wave recently, standing in front of that door that read, "Cacao. Drink chocolate." I pushed open the door, breathed in the sweet smell and the blast of air-conditioning, and ordered an iced drinking chocolate to sip while I studied the shelves.

Before, everything had seemed intimidating, but now it felt like coming home to a roomful of welcoming friends. Askinosie's farmers waved hello from their labels, Dick Taylor's boats offered to take me on a ride to Belize, Bar Au Chocolat teased me with its sensual Japanese-style wrappers. And an entire row of Patric bars stood tall, 14 hard-to-find varieties begging me to taste them, including a browned-butter bar that I knew tasted like the finest toffee notes in chocolate chip cookies.

But there were also so many new bars to try, names and labels I'd never seen before. I couldn't wait to rip them open and learn their stories. This happens every time I go to a chocolate shop: I see a new bar from a maker I love and, more often than not, a new brand that has just come to market. Sometimes it's a tiny local company, while other times it's a more mature company that has finally gotten better distribution so chocolate lovers like me can find it in their neighborhoods. In a few years, we could see the number of craft chocolate makers reach the thousands. On top of that, chocolatiers and confectioners are using this kind of chocolate too, raising the standards of their products as well.

In other words, there's no going back to industrial chocolate ever again.

I'm not the only one who thinks so. At Cacao, the store was bustling. A steady stream of customers ordered iced hot chocolates and ice cream and bought truffles and bars. Two ladies sat sipping classic drinking chocolate, undeterred by the 100-degree weather outside. A food tour crowded into a corner of the store to taste a few squares and learn what "bean to bar" and "single origin" mean.

"Taste the fruity notes in this Madagascar," the leader told them, passing around pieces of Woodblock Chocolate.

"It's . . . orangey," one person said in amazement. "There aren't any oranges in it?"

"Nope, just cocoa and sugar," she replied. "Chocolate has terroir, like wine."

I grinned. It was funny to hear someone else give the same speech I've recited a million times, to hear her talk about how chocolate is having a moment like specialty coffee or craft beer. The tour group's faces lit up as they got the concept and even more as they tasted the chocolate.

After the guide finished her spiel, everyone wandered around the store, perusing bars and picking out a few prime packages. Then, after buying them, they tucked them into their bags to enjoy later.

I winced. I could imagine each of them eating a square by themselves that night, an isolated indulgence that's a far cry from the fun of drinking craft beer at a bar or sipping espresso with friends at a café. I used to say that dessert was best eaten alone in your pajamas in front of the TV, but now I firmly believe that in order to get the most out of it, we need to enjoy chocolate together. A few years ago I visited Montreal, which apparently has a huge drinking chocolate culture: night after night big groups of friends hang out at local cafés, chatting and laughing with a snifter of chocolate (sometimes with alcohol added) by their side.

That's why in New York I started hosting the Underground Chocolate Salon, where a rotating group of chocolate lovers lounge around and taste chocolate together. I've always been jealous of Paris in the 1920s, when artistic and literary luminaries gathered at Gertrude Stein's house to talk and hang out: Picasso, Cézanne, Joyce, Eliot, Cocteau. Only one thing would have made it better: chocolate. I want the sentiment to spread. Recently someone told me my salon has inspired them to start a similar concept in the Netherlands, and groups have popped up independently all over the country, like the Manhattan Chocolate Society and the Utah Chocolate Society, in Salt Lake City. But we need to keep going. For craft chocolate to succeed, we need to create a new culture, a culture of sharing, and I want you to be part of it! I hope this book has inspired you to take up where I've left off.

That day at Cacao, I decided to make it happen then and there. I bought a few bars (okay, a lot of bars), then sat down at a table and opened them. I cut a few truffles in quarters, shot the shit with my friends, and took a bite of each bonbon and bar. They tasted like the future.

CHOCOLATE TIMELINE

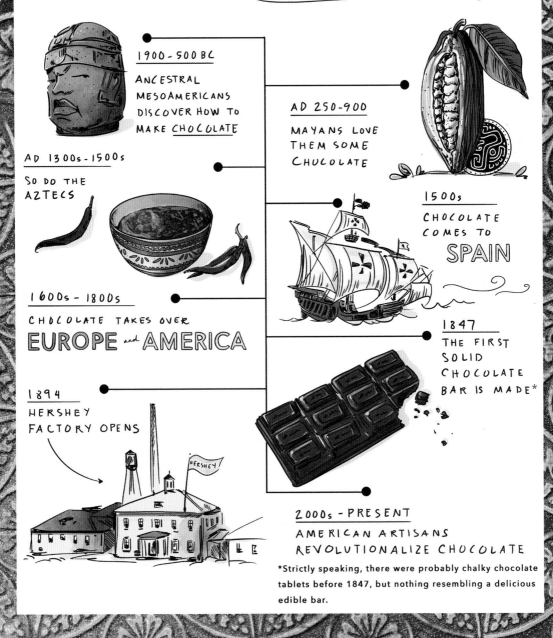

1900-500 BC

ANCESTRAL MESOAMERICANS DISCOVER HOW TO MAKE CHOCOLATE

AD 1300s-1500s

SO DO THE AZTECS

AD 250-900

MAYANS LOVE THEM SOME CHOCOLATE

1500s

CHOCOLATE COMES TO SPAIN

1600s - 1800s

CHOCOLATE TAKES OVER EUROPE and AMERICA

1847

THE FIRST SOLID CHOCOLATE BAR IS MADE*

1894

HERSHEY FACTORY OPENS

2000s - PRESENT

AMERICAN ARTISANS REVOLUTIONALIZE CHOCOLATE

*Strictly speaking, there were probably chalky chocolate tablets before 1847, but nothing resembling a delicious edible bar.

The History of the World . . .
IN CHOCOLATE

THIS IS A BOOK ABOUT PEOPLE. That's why I dove right in to talk about all the contemporary people making (and eating!) the best chocolate in the world. But people have been enjoying chocolate for literally thousands of years. Yes, thousands!

Let's travel back in time to remember the people who have influenced chocolate along the way.

ANCESTRAL MESOAMERICANS

Throughout the Amazon basin and into Mexico, ancestral Mesoamerican civilizations like the Olmecs first domesticated *Theobroma cacao* and discovered how to make it into chocolate more than 38 centuries ago.

MAYAN NOBLEMEN

By Mayan times, chocolate had become a vital part of society. In fact, the word *cacao* comes from the Maya. They drank it cold or at room temperature, grinding roasted cocoa beans on a **metate** and mixing them with achiote, chiles, corn, and water. If you've ever tried to mix chocolate and water, you know it doesn't work too well. That's why they would pour the liquid from one jug to another at a great height to mix it and create froth. The more froth, the better. The Maya even had special words to describe good chocolate: *yom cacao*, or "chocolate foam"; *takan kel,* "to roast the cacao very well in order to make a lot of foam on the chocolate"; *t'oh haa*, "to pour from one vessel into another from a height"; and, my favorite, *chokola'j*, "to drink chocolate together." The foamy tradition continues today in the form of whipped cream and marshmallows.

Both Maya and Aztec kings and noblemen drank chocolate often (in fact, there's a famous — most likely fictitious — story that Aztec king Montezuma would drink 50 jars of the stuff before visiting his 200 wives). But there's some evidence that regular folks had access to it too (though not always under the best circumstances, as you'll see in the following pages). When Europeans tried it much later, they found the bitter, savory drink disgusting: "more a drink for pigs, than a drink for humanity," one Italian explorer wrote.

AZTEC SLAVES AND WARRIORS

The Aztecs also highly revered cocoa. Once a year in the Aztec capital of Tenochtitlán, a well-chiseled slave would be chosen to impersonate the god Quetzalcoatl for 40 days, after which he would be sacrificed to the great god himself. The night before the sacrifice, the temple elders would tell him his fate, and then he would . . . dance! Yes, dance like crazy. If he didn't bust a move and/or seemed a little down, they'd feed him a gourd of chocolate to "bewitch" him. In the morning they'd tear out his heart.

The cacao pod was apparently a symbol of the human heart extracted during a sacrifice. To the Aztecs, chocolate itself was a symbol of blood, because it was so integral to their lives and quite possibly because it was literally dyed red from the achiote added to it.

Sacrificial slaves weren't the only ones fed chocolate. Chocolate drinks were also served to new warriors when they entered prestigious army regiments, which was thought to make them "blazing with spirit and courage."

CHRISTOPHER COLUMBUS

In 1502 Columbus sailed the ocean blue and arrived in Guanaja, Honduras, where he encountered a Mayan trading canoe with roots and grains as well as some "almonds" that the Maya used as money. He and his son (who wrote about the encounter) were surprised at how much the nuts were worth, since when they fell, the Maya rushed to pick them up, "as if an eye had fallen." Little did he know that these almonds were actually cocoa beans, which were used as legal currency by the Aztecs until around 1750. In Nicaragua, for example, a slave was worth 100 beans, a prostitute 8 to 10 beans, and a rabbit 10 beans.

HERNÁN CORTÉS

Cortés, on the other hand, recognized the power of cocoa, first as money and then as foodstuff. In the first half of the sixteenth century, he recorded a secret Aztec recipe, which included cocoa, sugar, cinnamon, pepper, clove, vanilla beans, anise, hazelnuts, musk, and orange blossoms (clearly European sensibilities had influenced the Aztecs by this point, since orange blossom was a favorite flavor in the Old World). It's rumored that when he traveled back to Spain in 1527, he brought cocoa beans home with him as a gift to the Spanish king, though nothing much came of it.

The Etymology of Chocolate

No one really knows where the word *chocolate* came from. Mesoamericans used all sorts of terms for their special savory drink, and some sound like *cacao* but none quite like *chocolate*. Let's follow the etymological tree that leads to the most important word in the English vocabulary.

Kakawa

A Mixe-Zoquean word used by ancient peoples like the Olmec in what's now Mexico.

Kakaw

The Classic Maya wrote a glyph for the phonetic compound *kakaw*, or cacao.

Chokola'j

The Quiché Maya word for drinking chocolate together.

Chacau haa

The seventeenth-century Mayan word for "hot water," where *water* could also mean chocolate.

Cacahuacuauhuitl

The sixteenth-century Aztec name for the cacao tree.

Cacahuatl

The Aztec word for "cacao water," their savory drink. The Spanish didn't like the idea of using a word that sounded like "caca" ("shit" in Spanish) to describe a thick, brown drink.

Chocolatl

A word that the Spanish most likely invented. Rather than calling the drink *chocol haa* like the Maya (a variation on *chacau haa*, mentioned at left), they replaced *haa* with a Nahuatl word for "water," *atl*, and arrived at *chocolatl*.

Chocolate

A word coined by the Spanish simultaneously and interchangeably with *chocolatl*. They drank it hot and sweetened with cane sugar.

BARTOLOMÉ DE LAS CASAS

So how did chocolate cross the Atlantic and get to Europe? No one knows for sure, but one story goes that in 1544, Dominican friars led by Bartolomé de las Casas brought a group of Kekchi Maya Indians to Spain to visit Prince Philip. With them the Kekchi brought all sorts of New World goodies to the court — including "beaten chocolate." Another theory is that religious clergy were captivated by the drink and its medicinal uses, and priests and nuns brought chocolate from New World monasteries and convents to their home bases in Spain. (There are actually many accounts of chocolate being made in Old World monasteries and nunneries.) Regardless, the first sanctioned shipment of beans went from Veracruz to Seville in 1585.

The Spanish added lots of sugar and served the drink hot rather than cold. They used *molinillos* to beat the beverage until it was mixed well and frothy, a holdover from the Mayans and Aztecs.

POPE GREGORY XIII

By the seventeenth century, drinking chocolate had bewitched most of (very Catholic) Europe, including Italy. It had become such an important part of life that people couldn't imagine living without it for a day, let alone on ecclesiastical fast days, when they were forbidden from, you know, eating. So was chocolate a food or a drink? Moral and nourishing or evil and aphrodisiac? The debate raged so furiously that throughout two and a half centuries, no fewer than seven popes weighed in on the issue. The first was Pope Gregory XIII, in the sixteenth century, who decreed that chocolate did *not* break the fast. The subsequent six popes vehemently agreed, nodding their papal heads as they ingested a tasty chocolate beverage.

BAYONNE JEWS

Surprisingly (nobody expects it, after all), the Spanish Inquisition was indirectly responsible for bringing chocolate to France. When Spain exiled Jews, a small number of them came to Bayonne and brought with them a passion for chocolate. These exiles took it upon themselves to make the first chocolate in France. The city quickly became known as the chocolate center of the country, and by 1856 it had 33 chocolate factories that specialized in Spanish and Italian methods, mostly run by Jewish artisans. The French became obsessed with chocolate and lifted it to new heights, transforming chocolate into an art, a tradition that continues to this day.

JACOB THE JEW

In 1650 a man known as Jacob the Jew opened the first coffeehouse in Oxford, England, called the Angel. Though called a coffeehouse, it served, among other things, chocolate, as at that time (mostly unsweetened) tea, chocolate, and coffee beverages were grouped together. Tea, coffee, and chocolate houses swept through Europe, providing a space to hang out, relax, and debate politics. In England the most famous were White's Chocolate House and the Cocoa-Tree Club, which boasted famous members like Jonathan Swift and, later, Graham Greene.

CHOCOLATE'S "SINFUL" ROOTS

Chocolate's dark color, strange allure, and reputation as an aphrodisiac have confused and delighted many throughout the centuries. The Marquis de Sade's biographer wrote that "chocolate inspired an irresistible passion" in him, and he was "capable of wolfing down frightening quantities" in all of its forms.

In jail he asked his wife to send him ground chocolate, chocolate biscuits, chocolate bars, and cocoa butter suppositories, among other things. "I asked," he wrote her in a letter, "for a cake with icing, but I want it to be chocolate and black inside from chocolate as the devil's ass is black from smoke. And the icing is to be the same."

In 1772 in Marseilles, long before he was jailed, the marquis supposedly handed out chocolate pastilles laced with Spanish fly (an herbal aphrodisiac) so that people "began to burn with unchaste ardor," a writer noted of the incident. Naturally, a chocolate-fueled orgy followed, with some people dying "of their frightful priapic excesses."

While the marquis embraced chocolate's dark side, it frightened many people, who weren't sure if chocolate was good or bad for them. In 1671 in France, an aristocratic woman wrote to her friend that a mutual acquaintance "took so much chocolate during her pregnancy last year that she produced a small boy as black as the devil, who died."

JAMES BAKER

In 1772 American physician James Baker and Irish chocolate maker John Hannon opened one of the world's first chocolate factories using power machinery in Dorchester, Massachusetts, where they ground the beans using water power. The first chocolate factory in America, it was called Hannon's Best Chocolate, and the company brand still exists today, as the now ubiquitous Baker's Chocolate.

AFRICAN SLAVES

As chocomania swept the globe, European aristocrats brought enslaved Africans to Central America, South America, and the Caribbean to work cacao plantations. Take São Tomé, where in the nineteenth century there were more than 100,000 slaves working cacao farms. European explorers also brought cacao trees to Africa, which, starting in the early twentieth century, became the world's main source of cocoa production. Generation after generation of African farmers have worked in poor conditions under a sharecropping system that would make Machiavelli squirm. It's still a problem today, with 70 percent of the world's cocoa coming from Africa, where farmers are paid as little as 71 cents per pound of beans.

PHILIPPE SUCHARD

In 1826 Swiss chocolatier Philippe Suchard invented the first *melangeur*, a machine used to grind cocoa nibs into chocolate liquor.

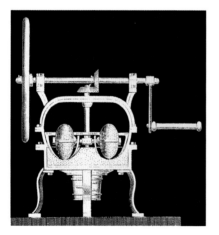

COENRAAD JOHANNES VAN HOUTEN

Chocolate changed forever in 1828. That year Dutch chemist Coenraad Johannes Van Houten patented a process for extracting cocoa butter from chocolate liquor (the ground-up nibs). The result was the powder that we know as "cocoa." Van Houten discovered that when he mixed cocoa powder with alkaline salts, it would combine well with water. In other words, he'd invented a much easier way to make hot chocolate, and alkalized cocoa — or "Dutched" chocolate — has become the go-to choice for drinking, baking, and pro-ducing mass-market cheap chocolate, even today.

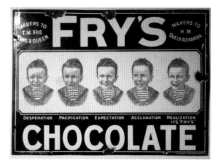

JOSEPH FRY

We think of chocolate as something to eat, not drink, but that idea is relatively recent: 1847. That year, in England, J. S. Fry & Sons made the first stable solid bar by combining cocoa powder and sugar with melted cocoa butter to make a mixture they could easily mold. There had been a few brittle bars eaten earlier, in eighteenth-century France, but this was something altogether new — and delicious. The company called its bars "Chocolat Délicieux à Manger," and by the second half of the nineteenth century, it was the biggest chocolate manufacturer in the world.

HENRI NESTLÉ

In 1867 Swiss chemist Henri Nestlé invented a process to make powdered milk, and in 1879 Swiss chocolate manufacturer Daniel Peter added powdered milk and cocoa butter to chocolate to make the first milk chocolate bar in history. You might have heard of the little company they formed: Nestlé.

RODOLPHE LINDT

Also in 1879, building on a design created by an Italian named Bozelli, yet another Swiss man, chocolatier Rodolphe Lindt, invented a machine called a conche. Conching stirs, aerates, and heats chocolate in a particular way to make it extra smooth. Lindt forever changed the texture of chocolate; before his conche machine, it had been gritty and coarse, but now it was mellow, smooth, and creamy. Conching became an industry standard, and even today Lindt is still a big name in chocolate.

MILTON HERSHEY

Called "the Henry Ford of chocolate makers," Milton Hershey figured out how to mass-produce chocolate, and the world has never looked back (well, until now). Inspired by a chocolate-making machine at the World's Columbian Exposition in 1893 and a trip to chocolate factories in Europe, Hershey sold his caramel company and started making chocolate bars in Hershey, Pennsylvania (named for himself), in 1894. His company imported sugar from another eponymously named town, Hershey, Cuba, until 1959, when political issues made it impossible. (Former Hershey's employees in Cuba still maintain his electric railroad with parts they've made and installed themselves.) A marketing genius, Hershey focused on the healthfulness of chocolate, and with popular candies like Hershey's Kisses, he soon became world-famous — and successful: today Hershey controls about 44 percent of the American chocolate market.

AMERICAN SOLDIERS

During World War II the US Army started including chocolate produced by Hershey in soldiers' field rations (they're still included in rations to this day). This particular chocolate was formulated so that it didn't melt easily in warm conditions and tasted "a little better than a boiled potato" so that soldiers wouldn't gobble it down but rather save it for a true emergency — not just a sugar craving.

GIANLUCA FRANZONI

On a trip to Venezuela in 1993, Italian restaurateur Gianluca Franzoni visited a cocoa plantation and became enchanted with the idea of making high-quality chocolate. In 1997 he sold his first bars, made with the highly sought-after Porcelana Criolla cocoa, and founded the Domori chocolate company. Along with French makers François Pralus, Bonnat, and Bernachon, Franzoni created the bean-to-bar chocolate industry, challenging incumbents like Valrhona and raising the bar for chocolate in general. Illy bought Domori in 2006, and the company still focuses on sourcing impeccable Criollo cocoa and making killer chocolate today.

JOHN SCHARFFENBERGER AND ROBERT STEINBERG

After studying at Bernachon, a chocolatier in France, former winemaker Robert Steinberg coined the phrase "bean to bar" and, with John Scharffenberger, in 1996 launched a company called Scharffen Berger that made high-quality chocolate bars. Their direct-sourcing methods, commitment to an intense chocolate-making process, and resulting flavorful chocolate revolutionized chocolate and influenced a new generation of American chocolate makers. In 2005 they sold Scharffen Berger to Hershey, which quickly moved the headquarters from the Bay Area to Illinois, laying off hundreds of employees.

JUAN CARLOS MOTAMAYOR

In 2008 geneticist Juan Carlos Motamayor mapped the cocoa genome as part of a USDA/Mars research program. The results shook the chocolate world: Motamayor found that rather than three types of cocoa (Forastero, Trinitario, and Criollo), there are at least 10 genetic clusters. (See page 63 for more details.) Since then the number has grown to 13, and it will continue to grow as we learn more about the mysterious plant *Theobroma cacao*.

My Top 50
BEAN-TO-BAR MAKERS
IN THE UNITED STATES

COME ON, ADMIT IT. I know you have a favorite chocolate maker. Everyone does, and opinions range widely. That's why I'm calling this list "*my* top makers." I'm not claiming that this is The Exclusive List of the best bean-to-bar makers *ever*; rather, they're the ones that I personally think are worth trying and visiting (if they're open to the public).

I've listed them in alphabetical order and divided them into tiny, small, medium, large, and giant — loose categories to give you a sense of whether they're a one-person operation or a 200-person conglomerate. Tiny generally means it's a one- or two-person shop without much distribution. Small- and medium-size makers have a few more employees as well as a retail location and/or café. Large makers have dozens of employees, a space where the public can visit, and good distribution. And giant makers have many employees (around 100), great distribution, and sometimes even wholesale or private-label businesses.

Find basic information about each maker below, and read more about many of them throughout the book.

Acalli Chocolate
LOCATION: New Orleans, Louisiana
YEAR FOUNDED: 2015
FOUNDER: Carol Morse
SIZE: Tiny
VISIT: No
PRODUCTS: Small collection of two-ingredient bars. All beans are sourced from a co-op in northern Peru.

Amano Artisan Chocolate
(see page 84)
LOCATION: Orem, Utah
YEAR FOUNDED: 2005
FOUNDER: Art Pollard
SIZE: Small
VISIT: No
PRODUCTS: Single-origin bars, especially from Venezuela, and some inclusion bars. Made with added cocoa butter and vanilla. Some private-label products. Provides to restaurants like Chez Panisse.

Areté
LOCATION: Milpitas, California
YEAR FOUNDED: 2015
FOUNDERS: David and Leslie Senk
SIZE: Small
VISIT: No
PRODUCTS: Large collection of single-origin bars.

Askinosie Chocolate
(see page 172)

LOCATION: Springfield, Missouri
YEAR FOUNDED: 2006
FOUNDER: Shawn Askinosie
SIZE: Large
VISIT: Yes! Check out the factory and shop.
PRODUCTS: Single-origin (especially from Tanzania and the Philippines) and inclusion bars as well as collaboration bars made with other artisan makers. Milk chocolate and even white chocolate.

Bar Au Chocolat (see page 186)
LOCATION: Manhattan Beach, California
YEAR FOUNDED: 2010
FOUNDER: Nicole Trutanich
SIZE: Tiny
VISIT: Yes! Check out the café and factory tours.
PRODUCTS: Two-ingredient single-origin bars, some milk chocolate, and chocolate-related products (granola!).

Blue Bandana Chocolate Maker
LOCATION: Burlington, Vermont
YEAR FOUNDED: 2012
FOUNDER: Eric Lampman (father Jim Lampman founded Lake Champlain Chocolates)
SIZE: Tiny, but owned by giant chocolate manufacturer Lake Champlain
VISIT: You can visit Lake Champlain's factory but not Blue Bandana's.

PRODUCTS: Two-ingredient single-origin bars with a few inclusion bars, chocolate chips, and roasted nibs.

Brasstown Fine Artisan Chocolate
LOCATION: Winston-Salem, North Carolina
YEAR FOUNDED: 2011
FOUNDERS: Rom Still and Barbara Price
SIZE: Tiny
VISIT: Yes! Check out the factory and shop.
PRODUCTS: Single-origin bars as well as inclusion bars with interesting ingredients like dried blueberries.

Cacao Prieto
LOCATION: Brooklyn, New York
YEAR FOUNDED: 2010
FOUNDER: Daniel Prieto Preston
SIZE: Small
VISIT: Yes! Check out the factory with antique machines and the small shop, as well as tours on the weekends and by appointment.
PRODUCTS: Single-origin bars, inclusion bars, couverture, hot chocolate, and nibs, all using cocoa from the Dominican Republic.

Castronovo Chocolate
LOCATION: Stuart, Florida
YEAR FOUNDED: 2012
FOUNDERS: Denise and James Castronovo
SIZE: Small
VISIT: Yes! Check out the shop.

PRODUCTS: Focuses on rare heirloom beans and single-origin bars. If you visit the shop you can also try and buy truffles, cookies, drinking chocolate, and more.

Charm School Chocolate
LOCATION: Baltimore, Maryland
YEAR FOUNDED: 2012
FOUNDER: Joshua Rosen
SIZE: Tiny
VISIT: No
PRODUCTS: Vegan bars with lots of fun inclusions and other products (think toffee almond bites).

Chequessett Chocolate
LOCATION: North Truro, Massachusetts
YEAR FOUNDED: 2014
FOUNDERS: Katie Reed and Josiah Mayo
SIZE: Small
VISIT: Yes! Check out the café with plenty of special desserts and confections.
PRODUCTS: Single-origin and inclusion bars and bonbons as well as drinking chocolate, nibs, and beans.

Cocanú Chocolate
LOCATION: Portland, Oregon
YEAR FOUNDED: 2009
FOUNDER: Sebastián Cisneros
SIZE: Tiny
VISIT: No
PRODUCTS: Inclusion bars with creative ingredients like bee pollen, Palo Santo wood, and Pop Rocks (see page 189 for a recipe).

Dandelion Chocolate
(see page 191)

LOCATION: San Francisco, California

YEAR FOUNDED: 2010

FOUNDERS: Todd Masonis and Cameron Ring

SIZE: Large

VISIT: Yes! Check out the factory and café.

PRODUCTS: Two-ingredient single-origin bars. If you visit the café you can also try brownies, cookies, and drinking chocolates.

Dick Taylor Craft Chocolate
(see page 145)

LOCATION: Eureka, California

YEAR FOUNDED: 2010

FOUNDERS: Adam Dick and Dustin Taylor

SIZE: Large

VISIT: Yes! Check out the shop and factory for tours.

PRODUCTS: Two-ingredient single-origin bars and some inclusion bars, as well as drinking chocolate and baking chocolate.

Durci

LOCATION: Wasatch Range, Utah

YEAR FOUNDED: 2015

FOUNDER: Eric Durtschi, founder of Crio Bru (a cocoa drink brewed like coffee)

SIZE: Tiny, but owned by large company Crio Bru

VISIT: No, but you can check out Crio Bru, its parent company, at its shop in Lindon and take tours there.

PRODUCTS: Single-origin bars made with added cocoa butter.

Escazu Artisan Chocolates

LOCATION: Raleigh, North Carolina

YEAR FOUNDED: 2008

FOUNDERS: Hallot Parson and Danielle Centeno

SIZE: Medium

VISIT: Yes! Check out the café.

PRODUCTS: Single-origin bars, inclusion bars, and bonbons. If you visit the store, you'll also find ice cream, drinking chocolate, and more.

Ethereal Confections

LOCATION: Woodstock, Illinois

YEAR FOUNDED: 2011

FOUNDERS: Mary Ervin, Sara Miller, and Michael Ervin

SIZE: Medium

VISIT: Yes! Check out the café.

PRODUCTS: Single-origin and inclusion bars, plus many confections, baking mixes, cookies, and more, available online and at the café.

French Broad Chocolates
(see page 150)

LOCATION: Asheville, North Carolina

YEAR FOUNDED: Café concept founded 2008, chocolate factory founded 2012

FOUNDERS: Dan and Jael Rattigan

SIZE: Large

VISIT: Yes! Check out their lounge, factory, and boutique with a huge collection of bars from other makers too.

PRODUCTS: Two-ingredient single-origin bars and some inclusion bars with ingredients like coffee and malted milk, as well truffles, brownies, toffee, and drinking and baking chocolate online, plus cakes, cookies, and more in the lounge.

Fresco (see page 38)

LOCATION: Lynden, Washington

YEAR FOUNDED: 2008

FOUNDER: Rob Anderson

SIZE: Tiny

VISIT: No

PRODUCTS: Single-origin bars that specify their roasting style and conching style, so you can get super nerdy about it.

Fresh Coast Chocolate Co. (formerly Just Good Chocolate)
LOCATION: Traverse City, Michigan
YEAR FOUNDED: 2011
FOUNDERS: Nichole Warner and Justin Manning
SIZE: Tiny
VISIT: Yes! Check out the production area as well as café and coffee bar.
PRODUCTS: Small selection of two-ingredient single-origin bars, drinking chocolate, and brownie mix.

Fruition Chocolate
(see page 118)

LOCATION: Shokan, New York
YEAR FOUNDED: 2011
FOUNDERS: Bryan and Dahlia Graham
SIZE: Medium
VISIT: Yes! Check out the big store in Shokan and satellite store in Woodstock.
PRODUCTS: Single-origin and inclusion bars with creative ingredients like corn, as well as hot chocolate, bonbons, caramels, and other confections. They also make milk chocolate and even white chocolate.

Guittard Chocolate (see page 111)
LOCATION: Burlingame, California
YEAR FOUNDED: 1868
FOUNDER: Etienne Guittard; run by his great-grandson Gary Guittard
SIZE: Giant
VISIT: No
PRODUCTS: Single-origin and blended dark and milk chocolate bars as well as dark, milk, and white baking chocolate, drinking chocolate, cocoa powders, and couverture chocolate for professional chefs. Used by many food manufacturers, restaurants, and chocolatiers around the country (and internationally), including See's Candies.

Harper Macaw
LOCATION: Washington, D.C.
YEAR FOUNDED: 2015
FOUNDERS: Sarah and Colin Hartman
SIZE: Small
VISIT: Yes! Check out the factory and store.
PRODUCTS: Uses beans from Brazil's Atlantic and Amazon rain forests in blends and inclusion bars with ingredients like Earl Grey tea and peanuts and pretzels.

K'ul Chocolate
LOCATION: Minneapolis, Minnesota
YEAR FOUNDED: 2015
FOUNDER: Peter Kelsey
SIZE: Small
VISIT: Yes! Check out their factory and shop.

PRODUCTS: Single-origin bars and bars with superfood inclusions like pumpkin seeds and maca.

LetterPress Chocolate
LOCATION: Los Angeles, California
YEAR FOUNDED: 2014
FOUNDERS: David and Corey Menkes
SIZE: Tiny
VISIT: No
PRODUCTS: Single-origin bars.

Lillie Belle Farms
LOCATION: Central Point, Oregon
FOUNDERS: Jeff Shepherd
SIZE: Small
VISIT: Yes! Check out the shop.
PRODUCTS: Single-origin and inclusion bars as well as tons of confections.

Lonohana Hawaiian Estate Chocolate
LOCATION: Honolulu, Hawaii
YEAR FOUNDED: 2009
FOUNDER: Seneca Klassen
SIZE: Tiny
VISIT: Yes! Call ahead for farm tours and factory visits.
PRODUCTS: Single-origin and inclusion bars made in Hawaii from tree to bar. Mostly available through a subscription chocolate club, but any leftover bars can be bought online.

Madre Chocolate
(see page 61)

LOCATION: O'ahu, Hawaii
YEAR FOUNDED: 2010
FOUNDERS: Nat Bletter and David Elliott

SIZE: Small
VISIT: Yes! Check out the shops in Honolulu and Kailua.
PRODUCTS: Vegan single-origin Hawaiian bars as well as bars from other origins and with inclusions.

Manoa Chocolate
LOCATION: Kailua, Hawaii
YEAR FOUNDED: 2010
FOUNDER: Dylan Butterbaugh
SIZE: Small
VISIT: Yes! Check out the factory.
PRODUCTS: Single-origin Hawaiian bars as well as bars of other origins and with inclusions, plus brewing chocolate, nibs, and more.

Map Chocolate Co.
LOCATION: Willamette Valley, Oregon
YEAR FOUNDED: 2014
FOUNDER: Mackenzie Rivers
SIZE: Tiny
VISIT: No
PRODUCTS: Custom couverture and single-origin and inclusion bars as well as hot chocolate, cold-brew chocolate, baking chocolate, and single-origin cocoa powder.

Maverick Chocolate Co.
LOCATION: Cincinnati, Ohio
YEAR FOUNDED: 2014
FOUNDERS: Paul and Marlene Picton
SIZE: Medium
VISIT: Yes! Check out the store.
PRODUCTS: Single-origin bars as well as milk and white bars, inclusion bars, drinking chocolate, and cocoa nibs.

Middlebury Chocolates
LOCATION: Middlebury, Vermont
YEAR FOUNDED: 2010
FOUNDERS: Stephanie and Andy Jackson
SIZE: Small
VISIT: Yes! Check out the café with house-roasted coffee drinks, milk shakes, hot chocolate, and bonbons, as well as special-release bars.
PRODUCTS: Single-origin bars and a few bars with basic inclusions like salt.

Nathan Miller Chocolate
LOCATION: Chambersburg, Pennsylvania
YEAR FOUNDED: 2010
FOUNDER: Nathan Miller
SIZE: Large
VISIT: Yes! Check out the factory as well as the on-site coffeehouse with chocolate and coffee drinks as well as savory entrées.
PRODUCTS: Single-origin and inclusion bars as well as confections.

Nuance Chocolate
LOCATION: Fort Collins, Colorado
YEAR FOUNDED: 2014
FOUNDERS: Toby and Alix Gadd
SIZE: Small
VISIT: Yes! Check out the café.
PRODUCTS: Single-origin and some inclusion bars. At the café you'll also find confections, hot chocolate, and more.

Olive & Sinclair Chocolate
LOCATION: Nashville, Tennessee
YEAR FOUNDED: 2007
FOUNDER: Scott Witherow
SIZE: Medium
VISIT: Yes! Check out the factory.
PRODUCTS: Stone-ground chocolate using brown sugar. Mostly produces inclusion bars and confections like caramels and chocolate charcuterie.

Parliament Chocolate
LOCATION: Redlands, California
YEAR FOUNDED: 2013
FOUNDERS: Ryan and Cassi Berk
SIZE: Small
VISIT: Yes! Check out their store.
PRODUCTS: Two-ingredient single-origin chocolates as well as chocolate syrup and drinking chocolate. Visit the store for all sorts of confections.

Patric Chocolate
(see page 32)
LOCATION: Columbia, Missouri
YEAR FOUNDED: 2006
FOUNDER: Alan McClure
SIZE: Tiny
VISIT: No
PRODUCTS: Single-origin, blended, and inclusion bars like triple ginger and licorice.

Potomac Chocolate
LOCATION: Woodbridge, Virginia
YEAR FOUNDED: 2010
FOUNDER: Ben Rasmussen
SIZE: Tiny
VISIT: No
PRODUCTS: Two-ingredient single-origin bars as well as a few inclusion bars.

Raaka (see page 130)
LOCATION: Brooklyn, New York
YEAR FOUNDED: 2010
FOUNDERS: Nate Hodge and Ryan Cheney
SIZE: Large
VISIT: Yes! Check out the factory and store.
PRODUCTS: Vegan unroasted (not raw) chocolate. Mostly produces inclusion bars with unusual ingredients like ghost chiles and methods like steaming cocoa over simmering wine.

Ritual Chocolate
LOCATION: Park City, Utah
YEAR FOUNDED: 2010
FOUNDERS: Robbie Stout and Anna Davies
SIZE: Small
VISIT: Yes! Check out the café with chocolate, coffee drinks, and pastries.
PRODUCTS: Single-origin and inclusion bars, plus drinking chocolate, granola, and more.

Rogue
LOCATION: Three Rivers, Massachusetts
YEAR FOUNDED: 2007
FOUNDER: Colin Gasko
SIZE: Tiny
VISIT: No
PRODUCTS: Two-ingredient single-origin bars.

Solstice Chocolate
LOCATION: Salt Lake City, Utah
YEAR FOUNDED: 2013
FOUNDERS: Scott Query and DeAnn Wallin
SIZE: Small
VISIT: Yes! But make sure you call ahead.
PRODUCTS: Single-origin and blended bars as well as milk chocolate and drinking chocolate.

Starchild Chocolate
LOCATION: Willits, California
YEAR FOUNDED: 2013
FOUNDERS: Ash and Brittany Maki
SIZE: Small
VISIT: Yes! Check out their shop for bars, truffles, and special treats.
PRODUCTS: Single-origin and flavored bars made exclusively with coconut sugar.

Taza Chocolate
(see page 72)
LOCATION: Somerville, Massachusetts
YEAR FOUNDED: 2005
FOUNDERS: Alex Whitmore and Kathleen Fulton
SIZE: Large
VISIT: Yes! Check out the factory and store.
PRODUCTS: Organic stone-ground chocolate in single-origin bars as well as inclusion bars and confections like chocolate-covered nuts and nibs.

TCHO
LOCATION: Berkeley, California
YEAR FOUNDED: 2007
FOUNDERS: NASA giant Timothy Childs and Karl Bittong; formerly run by Louis Rossetto and Jane Metcalfe, the founders of *Wired* magazine; chocolate is made by Brad Kintzer
SIZE: Giant
VISIT: No
PRODUCTS: Bars characterized by flavor notes instead of origin or percentage; tons of inclusion bars in flavors like astronaut ice cream.

Tejas Chocolate
LOCATION: Tomball, Texas
YEAR FOUNDED: 2010
FOUNDERS: Scott Moore Jr. and Michelle Holland
SIZE: Small
VISIT: Yes! In addition to chocolate bars and bonbons, they make barbecue, so come hungry.
PRODUCTS: Single-origin chocolate bars and unusual bonbons (think Parmesan cheese).

Terroir Chocolate
LOCATION: Fergus Falls, Minnesota
YEAR FOUNDED: 2013
FOUNDERS: Josh and Kristin Mohagen
SIZE: Tiny
VISIT: No
PRODUCTS: A few single-origin bars but mostly inclusion bars.

Theo
LOCATION: Seattle, Washington
YEAR FOUNDED: 2006
FOUNDERS: Joseph Whinney and Debra Music
SIZE: Giant
VISIT: Yes! Check out the factory and store.
PRODUCTS: Blends and inclusion bars in flavors like coconut curry and cherry almond.

Videri Chocolate Factory
LOCATION: Raleigh, North Carolina
YEAR FOUNDED: 2011
FOUNDERS: Sam and Starr Ratto and Chris Heavener
SIZE: Medium
VISIT: Yes! Check out the factory and store.
PRODUCTS: Dark and milk bars as well as confections and baking chocolate.

Woodblock Chocolate Manufactory
LOCATION: Portland, Oregon
YEAR FOUNDED: 2010
FOUNDERS: Charley and Jessica Wheelock
SIZE: Small
VISIT: Yes! Visit the factory.
PRODUCTS: Two-ingredient single-origin bars as well as a few inclusion bars and drinking chocolate. Used by Stumptown Coffee Roasters and many other restaurants and confectioners.

Bean-to-Bar Makers Who Sell Baking and/or Bulk Chocolate

Acalli	Chocovivo	Fortuna	Ranger
Altus	ChocXO	French Broad	SpagnVola
Amano	Coleman & Davis	Fresco	Taza
Askinosie	Creo	Guittard	Tcho
Black Mountain	Davis	Manoa	Theo
Cacao Prieto	Dick Taylor	Map	Videri
Castronovo	Ethereal	Maverick	Zak's
Chequessett	Fine & Raw	Mindo	

Farms, Co-Ops, and COMPANIES

WE WOULDN'T HAVE CHOCOLATE WITHOUT FARMERS. It's that simple. That's why it's important to give credit where credit is due. Here are eight of the most common farms, farmer co-ops, and private companies from which American makers source cocoa.

Akesson's Organic
LOCATION: Madagascar
TYPE: Single-estate farm
MAKERS WHO USE IT: Areté, Bar Au Chocolat, Dandelion, Fresh Coast, Guittard, Patric, Raaka, Rogue, Solstice
ON THE LABEL: Look for the phrase "Sambirano Valley" or "Ambanja"
DESCRIPTION: This massive plantation grows, ferments, and dries cacao itself. It provides beans to many makers all over the world, in particular in the United States. Banana trees protect Akesson's cacao trees, providing them with much-coveted shade.

Alto Beni Cacao Company
LOCATION: Bolivia
TYPE: Co-op
MAKERS WHO USE IT: Dick Taylor, Fruition, Parliament, Raaka, Taza
ON THE LABEL: Look for the phrase "Alto Beni" or "Wild Bolivian"
DESCRIPTION: Founded by Taza's Alex Whitmore and a Bolivian exporter and partnering with Invalsa coffee, this co-op of around 500 small farmers provides a place for centralized fermentation and drying, which vastly improves the quality of the cocoa. They've also planted tons of seedlings to expand the Bolivian cacao industry.

Camino Verde
LOCATION: Ecuador
TYPE: Single-estate farm
MAKERS WHO USE IT: Dandelion, Dick Taylor, Ethereal, Ritual, Rogue, Solstice, Videri
ON THE LABEL: Look for the phrase "Balao" or "Camino Verde"
DESCRIPTION: An intense, thoughtful farmer named Vicente Norero runs this farm in Balao, Ecuador, where he grows, ferments, and sells cacao beans. He approaches fermenting cacao as if he were making a fine wine, experimenting with different ingredients, times, and methods until he achieves the floral perfection that Ecuadorian cocoa is known for.

Kokoa Kamili
LOCATION: Tanzania
TYPE: Private company
MAKERS WHO USE IT: Areté, Blue Bandana, Dandelion, LetterPress, Nuance
ON THE LABEL: Look for "Kokoa Kamili"
DESCRIPTION: This social enterprise operation and fermentary oversees fermentation and drying for 95 percent of farmers in the area (more than 2,000 farmers!). By improving those two processes, Kokoa Kamili helps farmers get better prices for their beans.

Marañón Chocolate

LOCATION: Peru

TYPE: Private company

MAKERS WHO USE IT: Durci, Fruition, LetterPress, Ritual

ON THE LABEL: Look for the phrase "Marañón" or "Fortunato No. 4"

DESCRIPTION: This small company buys raw beans and ferments and dries them itself in the Marañón Canyon in Peru, where you'll find rare Nacional beans. The high-quality, fruity beans have taken over American makers' bars lately.

Maya Mountain

LOCATION: Belize

TYPE: Private company

MAKERS WHO USE IT: Castronovo, Charm School, Dandelion, Dick Taylor, Ethereal, Fresh Coast, Raaka, Ritual, Taza

ON THE LABEL: Look for "Maya Mountain" or "Toledo, Belize"

DESCRIPTION: A social enterprise company in southern Belize, Maya Mountain buys wet cacao beans from more than 400 certified-organic Q'eqchi' and Mopan Maya farmers and ferments and dries them. It also manages a 60-acre demonstration farm in collaboration with Maya families. Cool facts: Maya Mountain was cofounded by Taza's Alex Whitmore, and it offers microloans to farmers for training and equipment.

Oko-Caribe

LOCATION: Dominican Republic

TYPE: Private company

MAKERS WHO USE IT: Dandelion, Fresco, LetterPress, Parliament, Raaka, Taza

ON THE LABEL: Look for "Oko-Caribe" or "San Francisco de Macoris, DR"

DESCRIPTION: This company purchases beans from 165 farmers working more than 1,000 hectares of organic land. You'll find notes of tropical fruit and bright acidity in their cocoa.

San Juan Estate

LOCATION: Trinidad

TYPE: Single-estate farm

MAKERS WHO USE IT: Dandelion, LetterPress

ON THE LABEL: Look for "San Juan Estate" or "Gran Couva Trinidad"

DESCRIPTION: This single estate sold its beans exclusively to Valrhona for many years, but after creating higher-yielding hybrid plants, it found itself with a surplus of beans. That's great news for American makers, who have started making bars with cocoa from this shade-grown cacao.

Glossary of
CHOCOLATE WORDS

Thanks to Amano Artisan Chocolate, the Fine Chocolate Industry Association, and Ed Seguine for their help with these terms!

alkalization. The process of treating cocoa powder with an alkaline solution, which neutralizes some of the natural acids, reduces chocolate flavor intensity, and produces a less bitter cocoa that more easily mixes with liquids. The process was invented by Dutch chemist Coenraad Johannes Van Houten in 1828. Also called "Dutching" or "Dutch processing."

alkalized cocoa powder. Cocoa powder that has been treated with an alkaline solution. Compared to natural cocoa powder, it's a deeper, darker brown. It's a familiar taste for Americans; think packaged hot chocolate or, in expert Ed Seguine's words, "the essence of an Oreo cookie." See also *alkalization*, *cocoa powder*.

artisan. Traditionally a person who has apprenticed with a master to learn a trade and become a master herself, or a description of the products she makes. However, in the United States it's currently an undefined and shape-shifting word, used by makers and companies however they see fit. It's often seen as interchangeable with the terms *craft*, *small batch*, and, in chocolate, *bean to bar*. Every maker uses it differently, but consumers associate it overwhelmingly with flavor and being handmade.

bean-to-bar chocolate. A messy term without an agreed-upon definition. I define it as chocolate made from scratch by one company, starting with whole beans. This usually includes buying, roasting, grinding, and refining the beans in a single facility. Some companies may not roast the beans, and others may not mold the chocolate into bars themselves, but in both cases it is still considered bean to bar. Chocolate made from preroasted nibs or premade chocolate liquor is not bean to bar.

blend. A chocolate made with more than one variety of cocoa. Sometimes blending is done to control costs. Other times makers blend beans from different origins to bring out complementary flavors and create a more balanced chocolate.

bloom. A whitish appearance and chalky texture caused by poor storage or care. Sugar bloom is caused by moisture coming into contact with the chocolate; the chocolate will look dusty. Cocoa butter bloom is caused by poor tempering, faulty storage, or changes in temperature; the chocolate will turn powdery gray, white, or tan and feel soft and crumbly. With cocoa butter bloom, the chocolate isn't ruined; it can be remelted and retempered and will be good as new. With sugar bloom, you're out of luck.

bonbon. Candy, especially covered in chocolate. There are many types of bonbons, but the most common kind is the truffle.

bulk cocoa. Lower-quality cocoa with robust, often flat flavors (usually from the Forastero family). Used in industrial chocolate.

cacao. The pod and beans of the tree *Theobroma cacao*, as well as the tree itself. It's referred to as "cacao" until it is fermented and dried.

cacao beans. *See* cocoa beans.

CCN-51. A hybrid of several types of cocoa that is hardy and easy to grow but is widely considered to taste terrible. Used by big companies like Mars.

chocolate bark. A sheet of solid chocolate covered randomly with nuts, dried fruit, or candy and broken into bite-size pieces. Named because it looks like tree bark.

chocolate liquor. Ground-up cocoa nibs, whether in molten liquid or solid block form, without sugar. Not alcoholic in any way (sorry). It refers to the nibs being in a liquid state when they are ground. Chocolate liquor + any added cocoa butter = cocoa percentage.

chocolate maker. Someone who buys whole cocoa beans and roasts, grinds, and smoothens them into bars in his or her own factory (or some variation of that process). Think of a chocolate maker as an engineer, creating chocolate from the raw materials. Someone who buys preroasted nibs or premade chocolate liquor is not a chocolate maker.

chocolate mass. *See* chocolate liquor.

chocolatier. Someone who makes candies and confections (think truffles, chocolate bark, and so on). Most of the time chocolatiers buy premade chocolate, melt it down, and use it to make their own bars and confections. Once in a while they make their own chocolate and use that to create confections. Think of a chocolatier as a chef who uses a premade ingredient to create his or her own masterpieces.

chocolaty. An adjective used to describe candy that can't legally be called chocolate because it doesn't have a high enough percentage of cocoa in it (at least 10 percent) or includes fats other than cocoa butter, like vegetable oil. To be avoided, because yuck.

cocoa. Cacao beans anytime after they have been fermented and dried, in bean, nib, or powder form.

cocoa beans. The beans inside a cacao pod and the key ingredient in chocolate. Technically they're seeds!

cocoa butter. The fat in a cocoa bean (usually around 50 percent, depending on the bean). Cocoa butter melts at body temperature, which is why it helps create a luxurious, creamy mouthfeel and is often added to bars and bonbons. Chocolate liquor + any added cocoa butter = cocoa percentage.

cocoa liquor. *See* chocolate liquor.

cocoa mass. *See* chocolate liquor.

cocoa nibs. The broken pieces of the cocoa bean after the bean has been separated from the shell. The nibs can be eaten on their own or ground to make chocolate liquor.

cocoa percentage. The percentage of a bar that comes from chocolate liquor and added cocoa butter. It is not related to quality in ANY WAY. Every chocolate maker has his or her own secret recipe and uses a different amount of chocolate liquor and added cocoa butter, which is why, for example, one 70 percent bar can taste so different from another 70 percent bar. Chocolate liquor + cocoa butter = cocoa percentage.

cocoa powder. The powder that results from removing cocoa butter from chocolate liquor. It can be natural cocoa powder or alkalized cocoa powder.

cocoa solids. The part of the cocoa bean or chocolate liquor made up of nonfat solids, usually between 42 and 50 percent.

CocoaTown. A common brand of wet grinder that many bean-to-bar makers use to grind and refine cocoa beans and sugar. *See also* melangeur.

conche. The name of a machine and the process of stirring, aerating, and heating chocolate to mix, release volatile acids, and polish the chocolate in a particular way that makes it extra smooth. Standard in European-style chocolate but not American style. Rodolphe Lindt invented the conche in 1879.

confection. Candy, like truffles, bonbons, chocolate bark, caramels, and so on. Doesn't usually include baked goods like brownies or cookies.

co-op. *See* farmer co-op.

couverture. Chocolate usually used to coat confections or in molded bonbons. More cocoa butter has been added to it than to other types of chocolate, which means it has a creamier mouthfeel.

craft chocolate. A messy term without an agreed-upon definition. According to the now-defunct Craft Chocolate Makers of America, craft chocolate is made from scratch by an independent, small company (one that uses between 1 metric ton and 200 metric tons of cocoa beans per year and is at least 75 percent owned by the company itself or the company's employees). The main concern is not consistency but artfulness and deliciousness. Within the world of chocolate, the term is often interchangeable with *bean to bar*.

craft chocolate maker. *See* craft chocolate.

Crankandstein. A brand of machine used by very small-batch makers to crack cocoa beans in order to extract the nibs.

criollo. A genetic group of cocoa that is considered desirable, as many (but not all) Criollos have a mild, delicious flavor. Called a fine-flavor bean in the industry. One of the most prized type of Criollos is called Porcelana, which has all white beans.

dark chocolate. No legal definition in the United States. A form of semisweet or bittersweet chocolate, under the umbrella of "sweet chocolate." Can contain milk products (!!!).

dark milk chocolate. Milk chocolate with a higher-than-normal percentage of cocoa, usually around 60 percent. This allows for the depth of flavor of a semisweet chocolate with the creaminess and dairy element of a milk chocolate bar.

direct trade. A popular system among bean-to-bar makers in which makers buy ingredients directly from farmers. This means that they visit the farmers in person to see firsthand how they grow and process cacao, as well as helping to improve that process, which often translates to superior cocoa. Makers who use the direct-trade model develop long-standing relationships with farmers and pay them much, much more than the industry standard or even fair trade. Many keep open books and help the farming communities with humanitarian projects. There is no official direct-trade certification system.

drinking chocolate. A thick, rich drink made of melted chocolate, sugar, and water, milk, or cream. Not to be confused with hot cocoa.

Dutched cocoa. *See* alkalized cocoa powder.

epicatechin. An antioxidant found in cacao and cocoa. If you want to get technical about it, it's a phenol and part of the flavonoid family.

fair trade. Certification systems designed to provide additional income to farmers. Fair trade guarantees a base price for certified cocoa beans and provides farmers with a bonus for community programs like health care and education. Many bean-to-bar makers feel that there are too many problems with this third-party certification system and prefer to practice direct trade.

farmer co-op. A group of farmers that has organized and created a governing structure, including elected officials.

fermentation. A crucial step to making chocolate that helps develop flavors (it removes tannins and makes the beans less astringent). Raw beans are fermented straight out of the pod. Depending on the region, the beans are fermented in a pile in their pulp under banana leaves, in black plastic tents, or in wood or plastic boxes for three to six days.

fine chocolate. *See* fine-flavor cocoa.

fine-flavor cocoa. High-quality cocoa with more nuanced flavors (usually from the Criollo and Trinitario families, if you want to get nerdy about it). It's also more expensive.

flavanols. Certain micronutrients and antioxidants found in certain plants that may be beneficial. One prevalent type in cocoa is called epicatechin.

Forastero. An umbrella term that in the past was used to describe lower-quality cocoa. Many people in the past (and some in the present) considered Forastero cocoa to be inferior and to taste bad. Now the term is used to describe any cocoa that is not in the Criollo genetic group and is not a hybrid. Many are hardier and produce more pods and more beans than Criollos or Trinitarios, which means Big Chocolate — which is interested in high yields, cheap prices, and consistency — often prefers to grow cacao and breed hybrids from this group. The most prevalent Forastero cocoa is the Amelonado genetic cluster. Forastero is considered bulk cocoa, not fine flavor.

ganache. A smooth blend of chocolate and cream, often with butter or cream added. Firm ganache can be used as the filling for truffles and bonbons; pouring ganache can be used on cakes and pastries.

handmade. Strictly speaking, it means a food or product that is made by hand, without the use of machines. Since it's almost impossible to make fine chocolate completely without a machine (especially when grinding nibs!), the term is another messy one without an agreed-upon definition. Common stages done by hand are sorting beans, filling bar molds, and wrapping bars.

heirloom cacao. Cacao that has been designated "heirloom" by the Fine Chocolate Industry Association's Heirloom Cacao Preservation Fund because of its genetic qualities and superior taste.

hot cocoa. Alkalized cocoa powder mixed with hot milk or water. Often confused with drinking chocolate.

inclusion. An added ingredient that significantly alters the flavor and/or texture of the chocolate, such as almonds, sea salt, or dried raspberries. In other words, a fancy way of saying there's stuff in your chocolate.

industrial chocolate. Chocolate made in huge quantities, often using commercial-grade beans with vast amounts of sugar, vanillin, cocoa butter, and emulsifiers like soy lecithin to guarantee consistent taste and texture. Low cost and consistency are the primary goals.

lecithin. An emulsifier used in place of cocoa butter to thin chocolate, whether to make it easier to mold, to create a smoother mouthfeel, or to make confections.

melangeur. A machine that grinds cocoa nibs into chocolate liquor, most often using stone grinders.

metate. A traditional Mesoamerican stone table with legs that is heated from underneath and used with a smaller stone utensil to grind and liquefy cocoa nibs.

microbatch. According to the International Chocolate Awards, bars made where the capacity of the largest machine in production is 110 pounds or less.

milk chocolate. Chocolate liquor combined with sugar, milk powder, and/or cream powder. In the United States it must contain at least 15 percent cocoa.

molinero. "Miller," in Spanish. This can apply to a person who mills not only cocoa but also corn, chiles, grains, or anything.

molinillo. A traditional wooden whisk used to froth drinking chocolate.

molino. 'Mill' in Spanish.

mouthfeel. How a chocolate feels in your mouth texturally. It might be smooth, grainy, gritty, or waxy.

Nacional. A floral-tasting type of fine-flavor cocoa bean most often found in Ecuador. It's rare to find a pure Nacional, as most have interbred with other varieties at this point.

natural cocoa powder. Cocoa powder that is not processed with alkali. It looks lighter brown than alkalized (Dutch-processed) cocoa and tastes slightly more bitter but has more chocolate flavor. *See also* cocoa powder.

nib. *See* cocoa nib.

100 percent bar. A chocolate bar made with only one ingredient: cocoa beans. That means there's not even any sugar in it! Some might call it bitter and unpalatable, others the true essence of chocolate.

origin. Geographical location in which the cacao is grown.

PGPR. An acronym for polyglycerol polyricinoleate, which is made from glycerol, among other things. It's often used as an emulsifier in low-quality chocolates.

polyphenols. Certain micronutrients and antioxidants found in certain plants.

Porcelana. A prized type of extra-high-quality Criollo whose beans are white. See also *Criollo*.

raw cacao. Cocoa that has been harvested, fermented, and dried all below a certain temperature; many say it's 118°F (48°C), but there isn't an established standard. Almost impossible (if not impossible) to find. Most products sold as "raw cacao" or "raw chocolate" are not in fact raw.

single estate. Beans grown on a single plantation, or "estate." The beans can come from a single variety of cocoa or a blend of varieties; all that matters here is that they are grown on one estate.

single origin. Chocolate made using cocoa beans from one specific place, or "origin." The chocolate can be made from a single variety or a blend of varieties, as long as they're from the same location. Note that right now, *single origin* doesn't mean that the sugar and other ingredients in the chocolate are also from the same origin.

small batch. A messy term without an agreed-upon definition. Based on numbers from some of the larger bean-to-bar makers, I define it here as chocolate made in batches up to 550 pounds, using a variety of equipment.

snap. The sharp sound a properly tempered chocolate bar makes when it's broken into two pieces. Experts look for a good snap as a mark of quality chocolate.

soy lecithin. *See* lecithin.

temper. The process of heating and cooling chocolate to the correct temperature while moving and manipulating it so that Form V crystals form, which means it will have a nice snap, sheen, and mouthfeel. After this process, the chocolate is shelf-stable and ready to be used for confections or eaten.

terroir. The French word for "land." It's a combination of factors such as soil, landscape, and climate that give foods like cocoa beans, wine grapes, and coffee beans their distinctive taste.

Theobroma cacao. The botanical name for the cacao tree, a tropical evergreen. The genus name, bestowed on it by botanist Carolus Linnaeus, means "food of the gods."

theobromine. A stimulant related to caffeine and one of several hundred compounds that compose chocolate. Found in the seeds of the fruit of *Theobroma cacao*.

tree-to-bar chocolate. Chocolate made from scratch by people who grow their own cacao as well as ferment, dry, roast, grind, and smoothen the beans into chocolate.

Trinitario. A type of fine-flavor cocoa that's a hybrid of two types of beans: Criollo and any other genetic strain previously thought to be Forastero. The beans combine the disease resistance and more robust nature of Forasteros with the delicate flavor of Criollos. Named after Trinidad, their place of origin.

truffle. A type of bonbon made with ganache in the center and thinly coated in chocolate.

two-ingredient chocolate. Chocolate made using only cocoa beans and sugar. People started making chocolate this way in the 2000s, mainly in America, and in many ways this style has become synonymous with the bean-to-bar chocolate movement.

wet grinder. A machine used by many American makers to grind and refine cocoa beans and sugar. The most common brand is made by CocoaTown. *See also* melangeur.

white chocolate. Cocoa butter combined with other ingredients like sugar, milk or cream powder, and vanilla. There are no cocoa solids in white chocolate. To be considered white chocolate in the United States, it must contain at least 20 percent cocoa butter and no other vegetable fat, a minimum of 14 percent total milk solids and 3.5 percent milk fat, and a maximum of 55 percent sugar or other sweeteners.

winnow. The process of separating cocoa nibs from the shell. If you're really DIY, you'll use a hair dryer to blow away the light shells and leave the heavy nibs behind.

CONVERTING RECIPE MEASUREMENTS *to* METRIC

Unless you have finely calibrated measuring equipment, conversions between US and metric measurements will be somewhat inexact. It's important to convert the measurements for all of the ingredients in a recipe to maintain the same proportions as the original.

US	METRIC
1 teaspoon	5 milliliters
1 tablespoon	15 milliliters
¼ cup	60 milliliters
½ cup	120 milliliters
1 cup	230 milliliters
1 ounce	28 grams
16 ounces (1 pound)	454 grams

Selected Bibliography

Baresani, Camilla. *In Search of the Lost Cocoa: On the Road with Gianluca Franzoni to Unveil the Magic of Chocolate*. Milan: Edizioni Gribaudo, 2012.

Bernardini, Georg. *Chocolate — The Reference Standard: The Chocolate Tester 2015*. Forster Media GmbH, 2015.

Coe, Sophia D., and Michael D. Coe. *The True History of Chocolate*. 3rd ed. London: Thames & Hudson, 2007.

Gordon, Clay. *Discover Chocolate: The Ultimate Guide to Buying, Tasting, and Enjoying Chocolate*. New York: Gotham Books, 2007.

Gutman, Liz, and Jen King. *The Liddabit Sweets Candy Cookbook: How to Make Truly Scrumptious Candy in Your Own Kitchen!* New York: Workman, 2012.

Leissle, Kristy. "'Artisan' as Brand: Adding Value in a Craft Chocolate Community." *Food, Culture & Society* 20, no. 1 (2017): 37-57.

Presilla, Maricel E. *The New Taste of Chocolate Revised: A Cultural and Natural History of Cacao with Recipes*. New York: Ten Speed Press, 2009.

Prinz, Deborah R. *On the Chocolate Trail: A Delicious Adventure Connecting Jews, Religions, History, Travel, Rituals and Recipes to the Magic of Cacao*. Woodstock, Vermont: Jewish Lights Publishing, 2013.

Rosenblum, Mort. *Chocolate: A Bittersweet Saga of Dark and Light*. New York: North Point Press, 2005.

School of Public Health and Tropical Medicine, Tulane University. "2013/14 Survey Research on Child Labor in West African Cocoa Growing Areas." July 30, 2015.

Sethi, Simran. *Bread, Wine, Chocolate: The Slow Loss of Foods We Love*. New York: HarperCollins, 2015.

Yuh, Eagranie. *The Chocolate Tasting Kit*. San Francisco: Chronicle Books, 2014.

Williams, Pam, and Jim Eber. *Raising the Bar: The Future of Fine Chocolate*. Vancouver: Wilmor Publishing Corporation, 2012.

Thanks

I couldn't have eaten all the chocolate in the country — and learned so much about it — without help from so many people, especially my husband, Marcus Irven. Special thanks also go to my family and my agent, Allison Hunter, all of whom had to hear about craft chocolate ad nauseum for the past few years, as well as my ever-vigilant adviser, Manuel Rosso.

Thanks go to the entire Storey Publishing team, especially Sarah Armour, Deborah L. Balmuth, Paula Brisco, Erin Dawson, Carolyn Eckert, Hannah Fries, Sarah Guare, Alee Moncy, Nancy W. Ringer, and Mars Vilaubi. Outside of Storey, thanks to the one and only Casey Kittrell at the University of Texas Press.

I also couldn't have done it without guidance, help, and education from the entire craft chocolate community, in particular Shawn Askinosie, Brady Belinski, Matt Caputo, Mark Christian, Greg D'Alesandro, Steve DeVries, Clay Gordon, Bryan Graham, Amy Guittard, Gary Guittard, Michael Klug, Michael Laiskonis, Alexandra Leaf, Kristy Leissle, Aubrey Lindley, Jesse Manis, Alan McClure, Alice Medrich, William Mullan, Dan Pearson, Art Pollard, Maricel Presilla, Dan Rattigan, Jennifer Roy, Ed Seguine, Darin Sukha, and Eagranie Yuh. And a special thanks to Pam Williams and Alysha Kropf at Ecole Chocolat.

I'm also thankful to my expert tasting panel's taste buds, in particular those from Matt Banbury, Sarah Bovagnet, Christine Clark, Krystal Craig, Kristofer Kalas, Tess McNamara, Nancy Palma, Michael and Jacky Recchiuti, Lauren Salkeld, Linda Villano, and Jessica Weaver.

Last but not least, I'm thankful to all the craft chocolate makers. You have opened my eyes (and my mouth) to how beautiful and delicious the world can taste.

INDEX

Page numbers in *italic* indicate photos; numbers in **bold** indicate charts.

ADDITIONAL PHOTOGRAPHY